THE CHAMPIONSHIPS
WIMBLEDON
Official Annual 2002

JOHN PARSONS

Photographs by

CLIVE BRUNSKILL, MIKE HEWITT, AL BELLO and PHIL COLE

of Allsport-Getty Images

Editor
JOHN PARSONS

Chairman
RICHARD POULTER

Publisher
NICK POULTER

Director
STEVEN PALMER

Business Development Manager
PETER MERCER

Art Editor
STEVE SMALL

Managing Editor
ROBERT YARHAM

Sales promotion
ANNALISA ZANELLA

Photography
CLIVE BRUNSKILL
MIKE HEWITT
AL BELLO
PHIL COLE
WARREN LITTLE

Photo Research, Allsport-Getty Images
ELAINE LOBO

This first edition published in 2002 by Hazleton Publishing Ltd,
3 Richmond Hill, Richmond, Surrey TW10 6RE

Hazleton Publishing Ltd is a member of Profile Media Group Plc

ISBN: 1-903135-15-X

Printed in England by Bath Press Ltd

Colour reproduction by Barrett Berkeley Ltd, London

Results tables are reproduced by courtesy of
The All England Lawn Tennis Club

This book is produced with the assistance of Rolex

FOREWORD

The 116th Championships will likely be remembered for the achievements of the new generation of players. The average age of the four ladies' singles semi-finalists was 21 and for the men it was 22.

While it was true that nobody aged over 30 has won the gentlemen's singles title since Arthur Ashe in 1975, and the ladies' singles since Martina Navratilova won for her last time in 1990, it is very unusual to have such young players dominating the final rounds at Wimbledon.

Our eventual singles champions, however, are both number one in the world. Serena Williams won her title without losing a set and, together with her sister Venus (the defending singles champion), seems destined to take the women's game to new heights. They also teamed up to win the ladies' doubles title as wild card entries.

Lleyton Hewitt won six of his seven singles matches in straight sets, the exception being his epic quarter-final match against Sjeng Schalken where he missed four match points in the third set before finally winning 7-5 in the fifth, having himself survived break points in that deciding set.

Tim Henman, at the grand old age of 27, continued his remarkable record at Wimbledon by reaching the semi-final for the fourth time in the past five years and again losing out to the eventual champion. As usual, his many enthusiastic fans cheered him on and his match with Michel Kratochvil drew over 13 million viewers on BBC television.

Todd Woodbridge and Jonas Bjorkman won the gentlemen's doubles title — this was Todd's seventh such title and Jonas's first.

I very much hope you will enjoy this record of all the excitements of Wimbledon 2002, which drew the second highest attendances ever in the 116-year history of The Championships. The largest ever single-day attendance was seen on Wednesday 26 June — the day that witnessed the shock defeats of Marat Safin (seeded 2), Andre Agassi (seeded 3) and seven-times former champion, Pete Sampras (seeded 6).

I am sure you will agree there was no shortage of drama at Wimbledon this year.

Tim Phillips
Chairman of The All England Lawn Tennis & Croquet Club
and the Committee of Management of The Championships

INTRODUCTION

It is some years since The Championships began with so many major questions — some emotional, others tantalising — waiting to be answered.

Domestically, of course, there was the extensive debate surrounding the hope that Tim Henman would at last become the first British player, since Fred Perry in 1936, to win the men's singles title.

Three times in the previous four years Henman had been beaten in the semi-finals and in each case by the player who went on to win the final, Pete Sampras in 1998–'99; Goran Ivanisevic in 2001.

Could this be Henman's year? Opinion was divided. In his favour was the knowledge that in the months leading into the game's most famous fortnight he had made his finest start to any year in his career. His fourth-seeded position was also his highest.

Emotionally the case for the British number one was naturally strong, especially among those who believed in omens. After all, it was 25 years earlier, when Her Majesty the Queen was celebrating her Silver Jubilee that Britain last provided a singles champion, Virginia Wade. So why not a Henman triumph this time to help celebrate the Golden Jubilee?

'Wimbledon is in my home country and grass is my favourite surface' he said repeatedly in the weeks leading into the tournament. The only problem was that there were 'ten or so' other candidates, according to Greg Rusedski, who were equally convinced that the title could go to them and reality, rather than sentiment, is more often the key to success.

Top of that list of other contenders — and deservedly so as we now know — was the Australian, Lleyton Hewitt, who, once he had recovered from the dose of chickenpox which blighted his form at the Australian Open, had lifted his game step by step until he produced almost perfect form to beat Henman for the second consecutive year in the Stella Artois Championship final at Queen's Club, eight days before Wimbledon began.

Some were not convinced that the 22-year-old Australian, who had won the US Open in New York the previous September, was yet quite ready to win Wimbledon but he was clearly

Slazenger celebrated 100 years at Wimbledon.

Opposite: Tennis fans flocked into the grounds eager to see the exciting and unpredictable tennis.

the man in form. In the absence of Ivanisevic, who had undergone surgery to repair a serious shoulder injury and had to miss what he had been looking forward to as 'that precious moment of starting the Centre Court programme as defending champion', there was plenty of support heading elsewhere.

Andre Agassi had made it abundantly clear that, although now 32, he felt he was still capable of winning the title for a second time a stunning 10 years after he had done so the first time. At the other end of the age scale, there was much support for the silken skills of Switzerland's 20-year-old Roger Federer, who one year earlier had ended Pete Sampras's record-breaking reign as champion.

There was also Sampras himself. Yet although many of his peers faithfully believed that simply being back at Wimbledon would once more inspire his best tennis, others were fearful that his confidence would be at a low ebb after two years without winning a title anywhere, and a first-round defeat at the French Open would leave arguably the game's finest player in danger of further disappointment.

On the other hand, could there be a triumphant return after injury for Mark Philippoussis or Richard Krajicek? And what about the host of young South Americans who, word had it, were determined to prove that their skills could bring success other than just on clay courts? Quite simply the fight for the men's singles crown had not been so wide-open since the pre-Sampras days.

Among the women, though, the absence through injuries of former champions, Martina Hingis and Lindsay Davenport, had concentrated minds almost solely on the form of the Williams sisters, Venus and Serena, and Australian Open champion, Jennifer Capriati. Venus was looking to win the title for an amazing third year in succession but knew probably better than anyone that not-so-little sister, Serena, was in the form to snatch it from her and join that small band of players who have won at Roland Garros and Wimbledon in the same year.

The scene was set. This Annual traces the way a fortnight, packed with seeding twists and turns, unfolded on its way to providing two awesome champions.

The semi-final. Wimbledon 2001. After trailing by two sets to one, Pat Rafter fought his way back into the game. With a brilliant volley, Rafter levelled the match at two sets all and then embarked on a gripping fifth set. Playing the best tennis of his life and saving several break points along the way, Rafter eventually triumphed by taking the match.

True
passion forgets fear…
overcomes fatigue…
triumphs over
difficulties.

Wimbledon – The All England Lawn Tennis and Croquet Club – 24th June/7th July 2002.

Rolex Datejust.
Officially Certified Swiss Chronometer.

ROLEX

1

LLEYTON HEWITT (Australia)
Age: 21
Born: Adelaide
World ranking: 1

Having rounded off 2001 as the youngest player — and the first Australian — to end the year as world number one, the slim, supremely fit and fleet-footed right-hander had impressively maintained his reputation in the first half of the year.

Once recovered from the chicken pox which undermined his bid to follow up his triumph in the ATP Masters in Sydney with another major victory on home soil in the Australian Open, he returned to winning ways six weeks later and went on to win his first 15 matches on his return.

By the time he reached The Championships he had won three titles, including the principal pre-Wimbledon grass-court event at Queen's Club, where he beat Tim Henman in the final for the second year in succession.

'I still have plenty of room for improvement but also feel I am improving every year as a player on grass,' he said on the eve of Wimbledon, by which time he was the clear favourite within the tennis family, and joint favourite with Andre Agassi with the bookmakers. Renowned for his speed about the court plus his ability to hit punishing winners not just off the ground but also at the net, over-head and with devastating lobs, it was difficult to see anyone beating him.

MARAT SAFIN (Russia)
Age: 22
Born: Moscow
World ranking: 2

2

Marat Safin is a strapping young man, who clearly enjoys playing tennis and life in general. Some suggest he possibly enjoys the latter rather more than is good for his tennis, otherwise he would surely have added to his first Grand Slam success two years earlier, when he overwhelmed Pete Sampras, at a time when the American was still in peak form, at the US Open.

He should certainly have started the year by winning the Australian Open. He looked the best player of the fortnight going into the final but had one of those frustrating days when there was a clear lack of drive and energy in his game and he was deservedly beaten by Sweden's Thomas Johansson.

Although possessing one of the most lethal serves and most punishing forehands in the game, there remained a lack of consistency that had too often prevented him from reaching his full potential. On the other hand in his three previous visits to Wimbledon he had progressed further every year so he was clearly a major candidate, providing he went into all his matches in the right mood — something still not guaranteed.

ANDRE AGASSI (United States)
Age: 32
Born: Las Vegas, Nevada
World ranking: 4

Since Wimbledon 2001, Agassi, the 1992 champion and the oldest of the 32 seeds in the draw, had accumulated three more titles to take his career total to 52, plus a wife, former multi-Wimbledon champion, Steffi Graf, and a baby son, Jaden Gil.

Agassi, who had finished 2001 in the world's top ten for the 12th time in 14 years, remained convinced that, despite fading in the quarter finals of the French Open three weeks earlier, he was still fit enough and his game in good enough shape for him to add to his total of seven Grand Slam successes.

Had he done so, it would not only have meant that he had won at least one Slam for a fourth successive year but he would have equalled Bill Tilden's record in 1930 of winning the men's singles crown ten years after he had done so for the first time.

He had been a semi-finalist twice and runner-up once in the three previous years at the tournament where he had already played 50 singles matches, winning all but ten of them.

TIM HENMAN (Great Britain)
Age: 27
Born: Oxford
World ranking: 5

Since he was first brought to Wimbledon by his mother at the age of six, Tim Henman's ambition has been to win what for most players remains the most coveted tennis title in the world. 'I know I have the game to win it and I'm determined to do so one year,' he has repeatedly said over the years.

From the moment he saved two match points to beat Yevgeny Kafelnikov in the first round in 1996, two weeks after the Russian had won the French Open, the pressure from the public for Henman to become Britain's first male champion since Fred Perry in 1936 has been increasingly intense.

Three times in the four previous years Henman had reached the semi-finals and, in 2001, he looked to have been well in sight of a place in the final until rain intervened and spread his match with Goran Ivanisevic over three days.

Since then Larry Stefanki, the respected American coach who had such a positive influence on the careers of John McEnroe, Marcelo Rios and Yevgeny Kafelnikov, had become his coach and helped him enjoy the most successful first half of any year in his career. For British fans it was fingers-crossed time again.

YEVGENY KAFELNIKOV (Russia)
Age: 28
Born: Sochi
World ranking: 6

Yevgeny Kafelnikov, who for years had been playing more tournaments, singles and doubles, than anyone on either the men's or women's tours, had cut down on his tournament commitments, doubtless hoping that it would carry him into Wimbledon fresher than in the past.

Although two titles and one final appearance on grass at other tournaments suggest that there was no reason why he should not succeed on the surface, he was still remembered at Wimbledon more for losing a two-sets lead against Tim Henman in the first round than being a quarter finalist — his best performance to date — one year earlier.

He would probably agree that he should have won more than just one Australian and one French Open title during his career. When he first appeared on the scene, eager and with such flowing style, there were many who thought he would not only reach the top but remain there for some time. Nowadays, however, there are too many times when the head drops and careless errors mask the real talent within.

PETE SAMPRAS (United States)
Age: 30
Born: Washington DC
World ranking: 13

Although Pete Sampras arrived at Wimbledon without having won a title since that emotional Sunday evening in July 2000, when, in fast fading light, he became champion for a record seventh time, there was no lack of his peers supporting his view that he was still capable of adding to that total.

His commitment was unmistakeable. Twice during the previous 12 months he had changed his coach as he set his heart and mind on proving that his shock fourth-round defeat in 2001 by Roger Federer was not going to be the culmination of his stunning Wimbledon career.

Whether the man who, at the age of 14, switched from a double-handed to single-handed backhand, and had gone on to justify the claim he made to his coach at the time that he would become 'a right-handed Rod Laver', could rediscover his former glory was another matter.

His confidence had seemed shattered by an early defeat at the French Open, when the consistency with his once awesome serve was missing and the authority had slipped from his volleys. Yet no one would deny that if there was anywhere that could inspire another great response from the American, it was Wimbledon.

ROGER FEDERER (Switzerland)
Age: 20
Born: Basle
World ranking: 9

Ever since he had ended Pete Sampras's record-breaking run at The Championships in July 2001, the tennis world believed that Roger Federer was capable one day of adding his name to those listed on the trophy.

Had that time arrived? Throughout the year he had talked enthusiastically about making Wimbledon his principal target for 2002. After all four years earlier, as a 16-year-old, he discovered that he could play well on grass, by winning the junior boys' singles.

One had to think back to Stefan Edberg's successes in 1983 and 1988 to discover the last time a junior champion had gone on to win the main men's singles. There was a strong belief that Federer had the game and the natural talent to do so.

His progress over the previous 12 months had been significant. He had demonstrated that he was quite capable of becoming a serve-and-volleyer, even if he was not yet quite adopting the strategy when it was appropriate so often as he and his coach, Peter Lundgren, would like. The one question mark which remained was whether or not he yet had the mental stamina to succeed at the very top.

THOMAS JOHANSSON (Sweden)
Age: 27
Born: Linkoping
World ranking: 4

Not even the most optimistic Swedish tennis fans would have bet very heavily on Thomas Johansson winning Wimbledon. On the other hand, nor, in January, did they see him as a likely winner of the Australian Open but he still returned home with the title.

Johansson has always been one of the most determined, rather than the most prominent, competitors on the tour and, before his amazing triumph over Marat Safin in the final in Melbourne in January, he had not gone beyond the quarter finals of any of the four Grand Slam tournaments.

In keeping with Swedish tradition, except when they have painted their faces and taken full advantage of whatever the local brew happens to be, Johansson's tennis, like his personality, has usually been quiet and unassuming but seldom wanting in terms of steadfastness and efficiency.

On the other hand there was nothing reserved about the way he, more than anyone, killed off British hopes of at last winning another Davis Cup World Group match in Birmingham the previous September. That and his grass-court success in Nottingham earlier that year showed that he should never be underestimated.

This was the first year that Venus Williams, champion at Wimbledon for the two previous years, had been clear of college commitments and able to commit herself, fitness permitting, to a full schedule on the Sanex WTA Tour. It had been clear right from the start that she felt ready to soar to the top and do her best to stay there.

Despite unexpectedly losing to Monica Seles in the quarter finals of the Australian Open, she won her first tournament of the year on the Australian Gold Coast and then added three more titles in the next three months.

Yet there were also obstacles beginning to be put in her way. One was a recurring shoulder problem which forced her to withdraw from the Italian Open and which, from time to time, meant she was unable to unleash serves with their normal power.

The other, even more significant, was the way younger sister, Serena, was starting to flourish so that, by the time they reached Wimbledon, the pair of them were ranked one and two in the world, just as their father, Richard, had predicted.

VENUS WILLIAMS (United States)
Age: 22
Born: Lynwood, California
World ranking: 1

SERENA WILLIAMS (United States)
Age: 20
Born: Sanigaw, Michigan
World ranking: 2

Another prediction from Richard Williams, when Serena also joined the ladies' tour, was that ultimately he could see her developing into an even more impressive and successful athlete than Venus. In the months leading into The Championships, there was ample evidence to indicate that this had already happened.

Despite missing the Australian Open with an ankle injury, Serena returned to competition in Scottsdale and thereafter had barely looked back. There had been a couple of hiccups, of course, including a defeat by Justine Henin in Belgium.

On the other hand there had been those highly significant victories for Serena over her older sister in the final of the Nasdaq Open in Key Biscayne and then the biggest breakthrough of all for her, in the final of the French Open. All the indications were that Serena, with a bigger serve and even heavier hitting off the ground than Venus, could win Wimbledon as well. She was certainly the most formidable-looking athlete on the tour.

For most of the previous two years, Jennifer Capriati had been living in something of a dream world. Suddenly all the horrendous experiences she had suffered as a teenager had been banished by a wonderful run of success which had brought her three Grand Slam titles and given her a prolonged spell on top of the world rankings.

The transformation could be traced back to Wimbledon 2000 when, for the first time since 1993, she began to rediscover the fitness and form which had prompted experts such as Billie Jean King to predict, correctly, that she was a future world champion.

From the quarter finals at Wimbledon and the US Open in 2000, she progressed rapidly and struck gold at the Australian Open and French Open in 2001. In January this year her added mental and physical strength enabled her to outlast Martina Hingis in the searing Melbourne heat.

She went on to reinforce her fine start to the year by beating Serena Williams in Key Biscayne but then lost some of the edge from her game when she failed in her attempt to successfully defend the Roland Garros title.

Although Monica Seles had not won a Grand Slam title since she won the Australian Open for the fourth time in 1996, she had given up hope of adding to the eight others she had already won before her career was so cruelly curbed when she was stabbed in Hamburg 1983. She certainly remained one of the most consistent warriors on the tour.

In her last 13 Grand Slam tournaments before Wimbledon this year she had failed only twice to reach at least the quarter finals and had enjoyed another outstanding start to the year by upsetting Venus Williams in the quarter finals in Melbourne before losing to Hingis in a three-sets semi-final.

While no longer hitting those stunning double-handed groundstrokes on both flanks with quite the power and length for which she was so renowned, even those ahead of her in the rankings knew they still had to lift their game to its peak to be sure of fending off her challenge.

'I keep playing because I still enjoy it' had been her stock answer during the year whenever she was asked about retirement. One hoped that was true. Few deserve to gain more enjoyment out of tennis than this charming and intelligent player.

5

Kim Clijsters, naturally enough, was brought up on clay but Wimbledon has always been the tournament closest to her heart and ever since reaching the final of the girls' singles in 1998 she has often described grass as her favourite surface.

Owing to a prolonged arm injury which had been seriously limiting the threat from her serve, Clijsters seemed to have spent as much time in recent months watching her boyfriend, Lleyton Hewitt, firmly establishing himself as the finest player in men's tennis, rather than pursuing her own career.

Time is on her side but after making an impressive start to the year when she upset her compatriot, Justine Henin, at both Sydney and the Australian Open, it was a pity that her arm problems returned during Roland Garros and prevented her from making a serious effort to build on her form in 2001 when she went so close to upsetting Jennifer Capriati in a classic final.

At the same time she always appears to have such a refreshing, down to earth approach to both tennis and her life, that her long-term future still looked bright.

Like Kim Clijsters, Henin arrived at The Championships having struggled to some extent to make as significant an impact on the game as in the previous year when that wondrous single-handed backhand, which had already won her plaudits all round the world, helped carry her into the Wimbledon final.

It was only her second attempt and followed a first-round defeat in 2000, when she would still have been young enough to take part in the junior competition. Her rapid progress was not simply confined to one tournament. Her ability to make good use of the full court had also been a major factor as she had boosted her world ranking from 48 to 7.

For someone who appears so slight, she packs a powerful punch, as Venus Williams discovered in last year's final when, apart from the equally hard-hitting Lindsay Davenport, Henin was the only player to take a set from her. One setback to her Wimbledon prospects was that the virus which had at least partly accounted for her first-round defeat at the French Open had also restricted her preparations.

6

Few players have made a more dramatic first appearance at The Championships than this feisty teenager, whose life in tennis has already been colourful enough to fill several volumes.

She had hardly walked through the gates of the All England Club for the first time in 1999, as a 16-year-old, before she was causing a sensation on what was then the new No. 1 Court by beating the top-seeded Martina Hingis in the first round and going on to reach the quarter finals. The following year she went one better and lasted until the semi-finals.

Then came all the upheaval of her rift with Tennis Australia which led to her outspoken and quick-tempered father and coach, Damir, deciding that the whole family should emigrate again, first to Florida and then back to Yugoslavia.

For a while her career seemed marooned, with good performances one week all too often negated by early losses the next. This year, though, although she had won only one title on her way into Wimbledon, her tennis was back to the attacking, spirited style that demanded attention.

JELENA DOKIC (Yugoslavia)

Age: 18

Born: Belgrade

World ranking: 7

SANDRINE TESTUD (France)

Age: 30

Born: Lyon

World ranking: 10

This was Sandrine Testud's eleventh visit to The Championships. Hitherto she had never gone beyond the fourth round. The oldest player in the world's top ten, she would have been the first to admit that her prospects of reaching, let alone succeeding at that stage, were slight.

Her form in the first half of the year had been mixed, to say the least, and her status as one of the top eight seeds was due entirely to the absence of two former champions, Martina Hingis and Lindsay Davenport, who were both injured. Over the years Testud has been a determined campaigner, though without ever quite reaching the top level. On the other hand, her consistency just below the top grade has been impressive. During the three previous years she had never ended the year lower than 13th. Although she had won three tour titles in previous years, during 2002 she had struggled to maintain her ranking. The confidence of the 5ft 9in right-hander had hardly been helped by a first-round defeat in the French Open a month earlier.

THE CHAMPIONSHIPS WIMBLEDON

James Blake was the most comfortable winner on Day One when his opponent, Mariano Zabaleta, was forced to retire after two sets.

The unavoidable absence of Goran Ivanisevic, the defending champion, still recovering from four hours of surgery on his serving, left shoulder and Pat Rafter, the previous year's runner-up on temporary retirement, did nothing to dampen the excitement surrounding the opening day of Wimbledon 2002.

Officials originally decided that it would be an appropriate gesture to invite Pete Sampras, winner of a record seven titles, to open the Centre Court programme. Yet the best laid plans do not always come to fruition. With the American worried about a rib strain he had suffered 48 hours before the start of The Championships, he asked for his match with Britain's Martin Lee to be delayed a day.

As tournament referee, Alan Mills, explained, 'By the time his request came in it was too late to do that because it had already been made known that his half of the draw was being played on the opening day.' At least, though, they were able to delay his match from first to third slot and former champion, Andre Agassi, was invited instead to take centre stage for the opening Centre Court match.

Sampras, who beat the British number three 6-3, 7-6, 6-3, said the delay 'probably helped a little bit because in a situation like this every hour can help but the injury seems fine now and it didn't affect my game.'

Lee must have been hoping that his opponent's concern about his fitness would strengthen his chances of achieving a major upset. For most of the first two sets that possibility remained. The Worthing left-hander was serving extremely well and from his point of view the Sampras serve was encouragingly erratic, with an ace often being followed by a double fault or vice versa.

British hopes were certainly optimistic when Lee forced two break points while leading 6-5 in the second set but that was the precise moment when Sampras's renowned, instinctive ability to survive under pressure returned well enough to ruin Lee's prospects of joining the famous-for-15-minutes club.

As always there was a heavy focus on British performances during the first few days for depressingly familiar reasons. British involvement by the start of the second week,

other than Tim Henman, tends to be limited. Even so, there were high hopes this year for Greg Rusedski for, although he had only played one match between the third week of March and Queen's Club for various reasons, including a neck injury, the British number two had indicated as far back as January that all his training was focused on being in peak condition for The Championships.

Opposite: As Pete Sampras launches a customarily fierce serve, he offers a clear view of the precautionary taping he felt he needed to help him avoid too much strain on the muscles.

Below: Martin Lee's eye was firmly on the ball as he fought in vain to upset the former champion.

One down, six to go was the confident, though still restrained, mood he offered after he had done all that was necessary to clear the first hurdle with ample power and very little stress. Though unable to sustain the whirlwind start which brought him the first set in 17 minutes, he had every reason to be pleased by the way he dismissed Austrian qualifier, Jurgen Melzer, 6-1, 6-4, 7-5.

There had been momentary concern when Rusedski, who had been serving solidly, found himself stranded and broken when serving for a 5-3 lead in the third but he broke again to lead 6-5 and this time there was no hiccup. 'He was quite a good player' said Rusedski. 'You don't win the juniors here by fluke.'

Barry Cowan, the Lancastrian left-hander who had captivated Wimbledon a year earlier by taking Sampras to five gripping sets, again made splendid use of the wild card he had been offered by reaching the second round once more with a 6-7, 6-3, 6-3, 6-3 victory over Hungary's Attila Savolt, ranked 70 in the world.

Cowan, languishing at 236 in the rankings, was not allowed to take inspiration at changeovers this time from the Liverpool soccer anthem 'You'll never walk alone' but three successive breaks of serve, at the end of the third set and the start of the fourth, gave him an initiative he confidently maintained.

Elsewhere there was no such pleasing news for other British wild cards. Arvind Parmar, 24, admitted to being 'slightly disappointed' by the scale of his 6-1, 6-4, 6-4 defeat by Sweden's 14th-seeded Thomas Enqvist. Jamie Delgado became involved in a dramatic comeback when he saved two match points in a third-set tie-break against Nicolas Lapentti and then had four match points of his own before succumbing 6-3, 6-2, 6-7, 4-6, 7-5. Similarly, among the girls, Julie Pullin looked like providing some cheer when she edged out Slovenia's Maja Matevzic in the first-set tie-break but was then swept aside 6-7, 6-1, 6-4 and Devon's Lucy Ahl was well beaten 6-2, 6-2 by the 13th-seeded American, Meghann Shaughnessy.

Apart from Sampras, two other former men's singles champions were also on first-

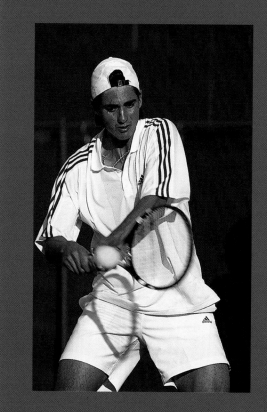

Top left: Jamie Delgado.

Left: Nicolas Lapentti.

Top: Julie Pullin.

Above: British fans supporting Delgado.

Right: Barry Cowan.

Far right: Greg Rusedski.

Inset far right: Jurgen Melzer.

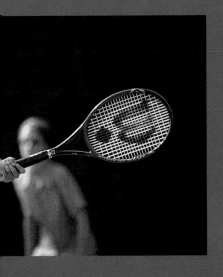

Right: Harel Levy.

Above right: Dominik Hrbaty.

Far right, top: Richard Krajicek.

Right: Agassi signs autographs after his match.

Above: Marat Safin.

Right: Yevgeny Kafelnikov.

day duty and the happiest among the trio by the end of the day was undoubtedly Richard Krajicek. While Agassi cantered past Israel's Harel Levy 6-0, 6-4, 6-4, demonstrating that his serving returns seemed to be as wounding as ever, it was Krajicek's return to the big time which created the most emotion.

Following 20 months in the wilderness, wondering if he would ever compete seriously again while waiting for a ruptured tendon in his elbow to heal, the 1996 champion dismissed Argentina's Franco Squillari 6-2, 7-5, 7-6. 'Three or four weeks ago my arm was still bothering me and I didn't believe I was going to play Wimbledon this year,' Krajicek said.

Initial hopes that he might be fit in time to have returned in Surbiton or Halle came and went. Then suddenly, ten days before Wimbledon started, the arm improved sufficiently for the 6ft 5in Dutchman to test it in Rosmalen. He lost to Roger Federer but the psychologically important first step had been taken so the call which many felt he would be obliged to make to the referee's office at the All England Club, requesting his name to be taken out of the draw, never had to be made.

Court 3 was packed to welcome him back and, though limited to 50 per cent of his former power and admitting there were 'still many holes in my game', he delivered 17 aces. He romped away with the first set in 27 minutes and saved the only three break points he had against him in the opening game of the second — the last of them with a low, beautifully executed, difficult forehand volley.

Krajicek was not the only menacing floater in the draw working his way back from injury. Mark Philippoussis, still down at 103 in the rankings following a second bout of knee injury, was also among the ten players Rusedski had listed as potential champions. Though a little nervous until he began to find the timing on his serves, he looked useful as he overcame Frenchman, Julien Boutter, 6-3, 3-6, 6-1, 6-2.

Agassi was given a huge reception when he walked out onto Centre Court and a standing ovation when he left only 1 hour 29 minutes later. The first set was over in 18 minutes. 'I feel great because the first one

Opposite: Another disappointing setback for Anna Kournikova as her second-set recovery faded and she was beaten by fellow Russian, Tatiana Panova.

Below: A pause for thought by Mary Pierce, back after injury, who was pleased to make a winning start against Alicia Molik.

can often be a difficult one you want to get out of the way' he said. 'I felt like I took care of the business nicely from the start,' and added that he felt 'honoured' to have been asked to open the Centre Court programme and thrilled that ten years after he won the title he was 'still in the mix'. Only once when he double faulted and was broken the first time he served for the match did his concentration wander.

Two men's seeds were beaten. Taylor Dent, the raw but powerful American who had pushed Lleyton Hewitt so hard the previous year, upset the 21st-seeded Max Mirnyi 4-6, 6-4, 7-6, 6-4 and Fernando Gonzales, the talented young Chilean who had made a

name for himself by beating Sampras in Key Biscayne, knocked out the 19th-seeded Argentine, Juan Ignacio Chela.

Few players create more attention that Anna Kournikova, the 21-year-old Florida-based Russian, who, despite reaching the semi-finals at The Championships when she was only 16, arrived at the tournament this

year still in search of her first title on the Sanex WTA Tour. Without doubt one of the most photographed women in sport, there must have been a thousand camera lenses pointing at her when she arrived on Court 2 and removed her tank top to reveal a bare midriff and a slit skirt which one writer described as 'more of a pelmet'.

It was only after the match started that anyone began paying attention to her opponent, Tatiana Panova, 25, the 22nd-ranked player in the world trying to forget that she had lost to 45-year-old Martina Navratilova at Eastbourne six days earlier. Running for everything, Panova swept through the first set 6-1 but, despite breaking to lead 4-3 in the second, could not prevent Kournikova at last finding the consistency to break back twice to level the match 6-4. A double fault, which broke her serve when the errors returned all too freely in the final set, eventually inflicted the third first-round Grand Slam defeat during the year on Kournikova, whose glum mood at the end carried over to a controversial post-match television interview.

With Kournikova out of the singles, the tabloid cameras switched their attention to Slovakia's Daniela Hantuchova, who had made striking progress since becoming mixed doubles champion at Wimbledon, not least by upsetting Martina Hingis in the final at Indian Wells in March. She looked suitably impressive in beating Spain's Cristina Torrens Valero 6-3, 6-2.

Mary Pierce, short of match practice after injuries, was pushed to 6-4, 4-6, 8-6 in an exhausting first-round match with the Australian, Alicia Molik, but it was plain sailing for two of the three players who had been placed out on their own by the bookmakers as title contenders.

Jennifer Capriati took less than ten minutes to sprint into a 4-0 lead against the Slovakian, Janette Husarova, and the minor irritation of dropping her serve was quickly forgotten as she took the opening set on her way to a 6-1, 6-4 victory. Serena Williams provided an even more emphatic start to her seven-match campaign and needed only 42 minutes to dismiss Australia's Evie Dominikovic 6-1, 6-1.

Above: Janette Husarova.

Below: Daniela Hantuchova.

Left: Jennifer Capriati.

Right: Jelena Dokic.

Below: Elena Tatarkova.

Below: Evie Dominikovic.

Bottom: Serena Williams.

TUESDAY 25 JUNE

day 2

Goran Ivanisevic may have been missing but his 18-year-old Croatian protégé, Mario Ancic, created the first major upset of the 2002 Championships. Playing not only his first match at Wimbledon but also his first in any Grand Slam tournament, the lean 6ft 4in right-handed qualifier, produced a stunning performance to upset seventh-seeded Roger Federer tipped by many, including John McEnroe, as the most likely champion, 6-3, 7-6, 6-3.

There were times when Federer, who may have underestimated the task ahead of him after breaking for a 3-1 lead in the opening set, looked utterly bewildered, unable to cope with Ancic's powerful onslaught. For all his natural talent it was another example of how mentally brittle the 1998 junior champion could still be.

Ancic was being hailed as 'Goran Mark Two'. If you closed your eyes when he was talking you could easily imagine you were listening to the 2001 champion and there were signs in his second-round match that he can also be as temperamental. Yet against Federer, who will always be remembered for bringing Pete Sampras's record-breaking reign at The Championships to an end in 2001, the talented teenager, coached by Bob Brett for most of the previous four years, was a model of concentration.

Only at the end when he stood punching his fists into the air while the Centre Court crowd gave him a standing ovation did the youngster, who had been runner-up in the boys' singles at Wimbledon in 2000, show any Goran-like emotion.

It proved to be a profitable day for several of the qualifiers in the men's singles. Of the 16 qualifiers and four lucky losers who went into the draw, eight of the former and two of the latter were still alive at the end of the first round, the others being Karol Beck (Slovakia), Gregory Carraz (France), Scott Draper (Australia), Hyung-Taik Lee (Korea), Radek Stepanek (Czech Republic), Nicolas Thomann (France) and Alexander Waske (Germany). The lucky losers were George Bastl (Switzerland) and Jeff Morrison (USA) but much more of them later.

Federer was not the only principal seed to falter. Australian Open champion, Thomas

Roger Federer (above) was the first of many leading seeds beaten in the opening days, upset by the 18-year-old Croatian, Mario Ancic (opposite).

35

Above: Tim Henman.

Left: Tim's parents.

Above right: Jean-Francois Bachelot.

Right: Thomas Johansson.

Left: Jonas Bjorkman.

Below left: Alex Bogdanovic.

Below: Lleyton Hewitt.

Johansson, seeded eight, was knocked out 6-7, 6-4, 7-6, 3-6, 12-10 after a marathon 4 hours 21 minutes by Brazil's Flavio Saretta, who was playing only his second senior tour match on grass.

Earlier in the day top-seeded Lleyton Hewitt had resisted what he expected would have been a major challenge from Jonas Bjorkman by beating the Swede in straight sets, 6-4, 7-5, 6-1. Before the tournament began, Hewitt had confessed to being intimidated the first time he stepped foot on Centre Court against Boris Becker in 1999 but judging by the way he moved and generally stayed in full control of his game and the match, even while fending off break points in the tenth game of the second set, such demons had become a thing of the past.

'It looked like being one of the toughest first-round matches and for me to come out and win in straight sets... I couldn't be happier. I've got more experience under my belt now and I've got confidence. I want to try and keep that rolling' Hewitt said.

Tim Henman thrilled the Court No. 1 crowd, and thousands more watching the large screen on what had become known as 'Henman Hill', with an impressively thorough 6-1, 6-3, 6-2 defeat of qualifier, Jean-Francois Bachelot. The Frenchman did not make the most auspicious start. It was a double fault and although he then collected the next four points to take the lead, the first set of what was to be a routine, one-sided contest, was over in 20 minutes.

Alex Bogdanovic, 18, the youngest player in the draw, looked for an hour as if he might cause an upset against the French Davis Cup hero, Nicolas Escude, who the previous year had beaten Hewitt in five sets. The teenager from North London hit rousing top-spin drives off both flanks to help him take the first set but the longer the match lasted, the more Escude's experience, and Bogdanovic's undue reluctance to venture towards the net, turned things round. Escude won 4-6, 6-4, 6-4, 6-4.

'If I'd just stepped it up a little more and had more belief in myself at the start of the second set' said Bogdanovic. 'Once he broke me in that set and moved ahead, he became much more confident.'

Alan Mackin, the 20-year-old Glaswegian who, like Bogdanovic, had been given a wild card to help him make his Wimbledon debut, emerged with much credit despite being beaten 7-6, 6-3, 6-3 by Jarkko Nieminen, the first player from Finland to be seeded. 'First they beat us at rallying, now tennis' opined Stephen Bierley in *The Guardian*.

As *The Daily Telegraph's* Andrew Baker said, the first appearance this year of Venus Williams in defence of her ladies' singles title had 'all the makings of a major road accident — innocent British youngster [Jane O'Donoghue] trapped in the path of a speeding American juggernaut and knocked aside mercilessly.'

In the event it was by no means so one-sided as the 6-1, 6-1 scoreline suggested. O'Donoghue might well have picked up two or three more games in both sets and played with a spirit, verve and style which earned the 19-year-old from Wigan, ranked 334 in the world, praise from the highest quarters.

'To be honest, she played very well' said Williams. 'You could see she had a game plan when she came out. She wanted to be aggressive and take all her opportunities.' And although O'Donoghue, who only began playing tennis seriously when she was 15, took only one point from the Williams serve in the first set, former champion, Chris Evert, said 'It's a long time since I've seen a young British girl play with such spirit on the Centre Court.'

O'Donoghue even broke the Williams serve when the top seed's concentration wandered briefly at the start of the second set, giving the Lancastrian who won enormous appreciation for her feisty approach from the crowd, at least one moment of triumph to recall.

There was rather less attention on Surrey's Hannah Collin as she faced Switzerland's Emmanuelle Gagliardi on Court 13 but the British girl was clinging on tenaciously against a vastly more experienced opponent until, in the seventh game of the final set, she slipped on the baseline and injured her left thigh. Although she continued with the leg heavily bandaged, she was clearly in pain and her worthy bid collapsed. She was beaten 6-1, 6-7, 6-2.

Jane O'Donoghue (above) impressed with her spirited approach against Venus Williams while Hannah Collin (left) took a set from Emmanuelle Gagliardi, and Paisley's Alan Mackin (below) battled well against Finland's Jarkko Nieminen.

Above: Samantha Reeves.

Far left, top: Brie Rippner.

Far left, bottom: Justine Henin.

Left: Kim Clijsters.

Below: Elena Baltacha.

The way things were developing, there was a horrible fear that Britain might end the day without any representative in the second round of the ladies' singles for the first time since that event was introduced in 1884. Then along came Elena Baltacha, the 18-year-old from Enfield, who suddenly blossomed in the manner her coaches, Alan Jones and Jo Durie, had always known was possible, to beat the much higher-ranked Venezuelan qualifier, Maria Vento-Kabchi.

'I've saved the day' joked Baltacha, who had spent most of the first four months of the year out of action, suffering from chicken pox, two serious attacks of tonsillitis and then food poisoning. At one stage she was ordered by her doctor to rest completely for a month. 'I didn't play my best tennis but I just kept on fighting. Even if you win ugly, a win is a win' she said.

Baltacha is the daughter of a former Soviet Union soccer player. Rachel Viollet, also the daughter of a famous footballer — the late Denis Viollet, a survivor of the Manchester United Munich air disaster — accumulated only 15 points against 19th-seeded Magdalena Maleeva, who had been just as fluent on the court as during her starring role in a television documentary shown the previous week about life on the women's tour.

After their performances 12 months earlier when Kim Clijsters was runner-up at the French Open and Justine Henin reached the final at Wimbledon where she took a set from Venus Williams, there was naturally much interest in how the 'Belgian Sisters', as Jennifer Capriati calls them, would fare.

Both won their opening matches though not with the assurance they and their supporters were seeking. Clijsters, who had been troubled by a shoulder strain for much of the previous 12 months, still managed to launch some thunderous serves in her 6-2, 7-6 defeat of Samantha Reeves but admitted 'It was definitely not my best tennis even if it was good enough to go through.'

Much the same could have been said of Justine Henin's 6-2, 6-7, 6-1 victory against Brie Rippner, the world number 74. 'My goal today was just to win and I achieved it' said Henin, who admitted she had been nervous coming into the tournament because of her early defeat in Paris and a virus infection had restricted her preparations.

There were no such problems for fourth-seeded Monica Seles. Though looking some way short of full fitness, the Yugoslav-born American achieved what was to be the only double bagel (6-0, 6-0) of the fortnight when she trounced Spain's Eva Bes, in a mere 38 minutes and that despite, vocally at least, struggling with a cold!

WEDNESDAY 26 JUNE

day 3

'I don't believe this is happening to me' seems to be the reaction from Pete Sampras as lucky loser George Bastl runs down another of his shots.

It is unlikely that any of the record 42,457 spectators who poured into the All England Club on Day Three and witnessed the extraordinary demise of so many top names, including former champions, Pete Sampras and Andre Agassi, had ever seen anything like it at The Championships.

No less than 12 seeds, seven men and five women, were beaten. Indeed in less than four dramatic hours spanning mid- to late afternoon, second-seeded Marat Safin, third-seeded Agassi and sixth-seeded Sampras were felled and, in the case of the latter, by a lucky loser from the qualifying.

By chance it was also the Centre Court's 80th birthday. The famous arena, looking wonderfully spick and span after its refurbishment, since Wimbledon last year, had been officially opened by HRH King George V on the first day of The Championships on Monday 26 June 1922.

Although rain delayed the start of play, the tarpaulin was eventually removed at 3.45 pm. Britain's Leslie Godfree, whose future wife, Kitty, was to win the ladies' singles title two years later, served the first ball to Algernon Kingscote, who netted the return. Godfree then raced to the net and pocketed the ball as a memento of the historic occasion.

Exciting as that must have been at the time, it surely could not compare with the events of 26 June 2002, which left the men's singles draw with only three of the top eight seeds in the third round for the first time since full seeding began in 1927.

As Greg Rusedski observed after he wobbled for a while against the Korean, Hyung-Taik Lee, in the one section of the draw where all four seeds came through, 'I can never remember having three such big names knocked out as early as the first Wednesday, especially former champions, Agassi and Sampras. It's created a real buzz of excitement.'

While in pure tennis terms the manner of Agassi's overwhelming 6-4, 7-6, 6-2, defeat by 67th-ranked Paradorn Srichaphan was arguably the biggest surprise, it was Sampras's unbelievably premature loss to 145-ranked George Bastl, a lucky loser from Switzerland, which made the biggest impact.

Sampras was close to tears after suffering not just his earliest defeat at Wimbledon in 11 years but the indignity of losing in a Grand Slam to an opponent who only a week earlier had been beaten by Alexander Waske of Germany in the third round of qualifying. Even so, Sampras left refusing to accept that his major tennis days were bound to be over.

'You have your highs and lows and this is definitely a low point' said Sampras, who had tried in vain to draw sustained inspiration from the notes his wife had given him to read at changeovers, designed to remind him of his abilities and her faith in him. 'I'm not going to give in to the critics, I'm going to stop on my own terms, not when someone else thinks so' he said. 'It's no fun losing but I still believe I have another major in me. I want to continue playing.

'I'm not going to let my time here end like this' added the 30-year-old American, rated by many as the greatest of this or any generation, as he strove to come to terms with his 6-3, 6-2, 4-6, 3-6, 6-4 defeat by Bastl, who before the previous week had never won a match on grass or on the main tour.

'It was a tough loss for me last year' said Sampras, recalling how his record-breaking reign had been brought to an end in the fourth round by another Swiss player, Roger Federer, 'and it's a tough loss this time.' While Bastl, who had only been third in line for a lucky loser place was mentally pinching himself, especially as Sampras had only been one point away from being in a position to serve out for the match at 5-3 in the fifth, there was a gasp over in Centre Court as the score from Court 2 was flashed up on the screen.

Although he recovered from two sets down to force a fifth-set decider, making his ultimate defeat even more unexpected, Sampras seldom dragged his game into an effective groove. For much of the match his tally of double faults outnumbered his aces. For more than two minutes at the end he sat on his court-side chair, staring at his racket but probably seeing no more than a void.

He eventually dragged himself to his feet and slowly walked off the court known as the graveyard of the champions, just about

day 3 • agassi v srichaphan

Andre Agassi joined Pete Sampras in a stunning second-round defeat, unable to stem the enthusiastic all-out attacking skills of Thailand's Paradorn Srichaphan (opposite).

managing to raise one arm in salute to a crowd which was on its feet paying what many believed might prove to be their final Wimbledon tribute to him.

Sampras, whose serving and volleying was a shadow of the immaculate authority one had come to expect, admitted that while he was still sitting there, minutes after Bastl had departed, he felt 'numb' and added 'It's not a feeling that I like, especially here.'

Agassi, the only player since Rod Laver to win all four of the Grand Slam tournaments,

was comprehensively outplayed by Srichaphan, once he lost a 3-1 lead in the first set. 'It was a bit of a shocker for me today' the former champion admitted. 'I never found my rhythm. I never settled in but there are no excuses.'

He was beaten handily by an overjoyed Srichaphan who had played the finest match of his life. Afterwards he put his hands together, with head bowed in silent prayer. 'I was saying thank you. It is part of Thai culture. I'm a Buddhist so I pray after a match.'

Meanwhile Olivier Rochus, at 5ft 5in, the

shortest player in the men's singles, was walking taller than most after hustling out Safin on Centre Court. Chasing everything in sight, unlike the Russian, whose form was too often lackadaisical, the Belgian produced a far greater variety of winners to complete a 6-2, 6-4, 3-6, 7-6 victory. It was sweet revenge for his five-set defeat by Safin in the French Open.

While Rochus scampered cheerfully and profitably around the court, more often than not picking the right spot to put away winners, Safin's game was littered with errors and no convincing indication that he truly minded. 'A bad day at the office' he said, offering a cliché that was as tired as his tennis. Although Safin had struck 21 aces by the time the fourth set reached a tie-break, 'Goliath' had returned little more than 50 per cent of 'David's' serves, even though many were below 90 mph. In many ways the fourth-set tie-break encapsulated the pattern of the match. Safin, who had lapsed back into errors after his recovery in the third set, hit a tame forehand to miss the first point, double faulted on the second and seemed to accept there was no way back.

The ill-chosen drop shot that gave Rochus a 4-1 lead was followed two points later by the last of many half-volley shots into mid-court and Rochus pounced on it to hit the winner with joyous enthusiasm.

At least the third former champion, Richard Krajicek, escaped unscathed on this remarkable day, as he fought off a thrilling comeback by the American James Blake to win 6-3, 6-4, 3-6, 4-6, 11-9. The match, which lasted 3 hours 7 minutes, followed Sampras v. Bastl on Court 2 but the Dutchman, who hit 32 aces, demonstrated that top names can win there, unlike Jimmy Connors in 1982–'83, Michael Stich in 1994, Agassi in 1996 and now Sampras.

Krajicek was thrilled by his success though he was so exhausted that the following day, instead of practising, he eased his weary limbs by going for a leisurely swim.

Also licking his lips in the belief that his chances had been strengthened by the day's events was Mark Philippoussis, who sent down 30 aces to dismiss 14th-seeded Thomas Enqvist 7-5, 6-3, 6-4.

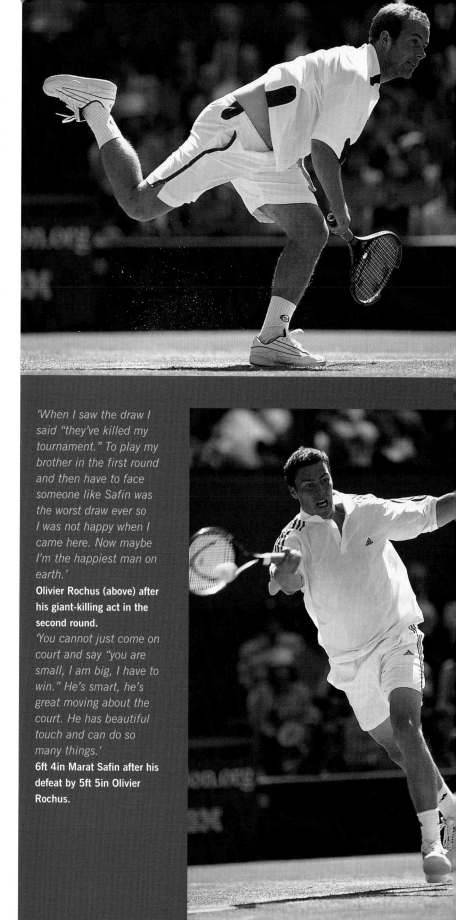

'When I saw the draw I said "they've killed my tournament." To play my brother in the first round and then have to face someone like Safin was the worst draw ever so I was not happy when I came here. Now maybe I'm the happiest man on earth.'
Olivier Rochus (above) after his giant-killing act in the second round.
'You cannot just come on court and say "you are small, I am big, I have to win." He's smart, he's great moving about the court. He has beautiful touch and can do so many things.'
6ft 4in Marat Safin after his defeat by 5ft 5in Olivier Rochus.

Despite his long lay-off it did not take Richard Krajicek (left) long to rediscover the required range and power on his serve as he won a marathon five-set contest against James Blake (below).

Back on the home front, where Rusedski pocketed the first set of his 6-1, 6-4, 5-7, 6-2 victory over Lee in 25 minutes, Barry Cowan, the only one among six British wild cards to reach the second round, began brightly and boldly against Nicolas Lapentti on Court 3 but slipped to a 4-6, 6-4, 6-3, 6-2 defeat. 'Obviously I'm disappointed,' he said. 'When you're playing someone of Lapentti's class you need to stamp on them. Instead I gave the initiative back to him' said the left-hander, who two days later announced his competitive retirement.

For the second day in succession, the ladies had been forced to take a back seat, even though Serena Williams was a shade fortunate to get away with as comprehensive a victory as 6-3, 6-3 over the little-known Italian, Francesca Schiavone.

'I don't think I was focused enough' said Williams, who not only scattered errors round the court but, like her older sister, Venus, the day before, costume jewellery. Venus had lost an earring on Centre Court. Serena shed a sparkling hairgrip in mid-rally and then lost the point and her serve when the point was replayed.

Jennifer Capriati cantered on, dropping her serve just once in a 6-2, 6-1 defeat of the Spaniard, Marta Marrero. Jelena Dokic, on the other hand, went to within two points of a dramatic loss against Kveta Hrdlickova. All went well for Dokic as she pounded her way through the first set with barely a peep from her opponent but her mistakes early in the second transformed the mood of both players and Dokic said 'I thought I was going to lose' after edging home 6-0, 4-6, 8-6. 'I was mentally down when she broke me at 5-5 in the final set. I've lost to her before.'

Daniela Hantuchova also went perilously close to an early exit. The 11th-seeded Slovakian had to recover from a break down in the final set against compatriot, Martina Sucha before producing enough booming forehands to win 6-2, 4-6, 6-3.

The highest seed among the ladies to fall was eighth-listed Sandrine Testud who lost to fellow French player, Mary Pierce, who would surely have been seeded but for her long period of inactivity in the previous 12 months due to injury. One break in each set was sufficient to give Pierce a 6-3, 6-4 win, her sixth in seven matches against Testud.

The picturesque scene above on Court 13 when Mary Pierce (left) was on her way to beating fellow French player, Sandrine Testud (left, centre).

Top left: Marta Merrero was beaten by Jennifer Capriati.

Far left: Jelena Dokic was pushed almost to the limit before overcoming Kveta Hrdlickova.

THURSDAY 27 JUNE

day 4

Following the extraordinary upsets of the day before, even the loss of a set by Tim Henman was enough to alarm the packed crowd on Centre Court and the thousands more packed tight on 'The Hill'. Then 80 minutes later after Henman had responded magnificently to what proved to be no more than a hiccup against Scott Draper, both areas were a sea of flags as the British number one completed his reassuring 3-6, 6-3, 6-4, 6-3 victory.

On his third match point, after the 28-year-old Australian had defiantly saved the first two, Henman delivered the brilliant cross-court backhand that prompted the noisy, colourful celebrations. It was the second encouraging British triumph of the day for, earlier, Elena Baltacha had upset 32nd-seeded Amanda Coetzer to become the first British player to beat a seed in the ladies' singles since Sam Smith defeated former champion, Conchita Martinez, in 1998.

Henman, by now one of only five seeds from the original 16 in the top half of the draw, was unsurprisingly not entirely happy with the way he played against Draper. 'I was never totally comfortable with my game. I'm still not playing so well as I would like to but I'm still in it. That's the important thing' he insisted.

He conceded that there was an element of anxiety when he lost the opening set, especially after what had happened the previous day and he was full of praise for the way the crowd rallied to his support when it was most needed and helped him turn the match around. 'They were very involved and I know from experience how positive that can be. You have to take advantage of everything you can. When I was down a set it was not looking pretty, I needed a lift and they gave it to me.'

The start by Henman had been efficient enough. In between holding his first two service games to love, his backhands did enough damage to give him a 3-1 lead. Yet the mood changed ominously two games later. He was fooled by a hooked backhand which dropped in to make it 0-30 and then overhit a couple of backhands to hand back the initiative.

For a while Draper, a former Stella Artois champion at Queen's Club and junior doubles

champion at Wimbledon in 1992, looked sharper, especially as Henman's volleying was letting him down and, by the time the set was over, he had lost five games in succession.

'We both had early jitters but I don't see any glaring problems for him or weaknesses in his game' said Draper, whose command effectively ended once he was broken in the opening game of the second set. The most crucial moment for Henman was when he held to take the marathon tenth game of the third set in which there were six deuces. Draper had three break points before Henman finally took it on his fourth set point. 'Tim got out of it at the start of the second set, the crowd got behind him and the whirlwind went on' reflected Draper.

There was no danger of Lleyton Hewitt joining the ranks of the first-week departures, although he had to work harder than most would have expected to fend off a resilient, albeit probably hopeless, challenge by qualifier, Gregory Carraz. The score, 6-4, 7-6, 6-2 duly reflected the way the 6ft 3in Frenchman with nothing to lose was prepared to give it his all. In the second set, especially, he matched Hewitt in the baseline rallies. The world champion certainly knew he could have been in trouble had he dropped his guard and needed those feather-like angled volleys which reminded everyone that he was the world number one.

Not that the day was entirely free from upsets in the men's singles. In a year when even Tim Henman was being more modest than in the past about being a serve-and-volleyer, Jeff Morrison, a 23-year-old lucky loser from West Virginia burst onto the Centre Court stage and showed that the art is not quite dead. He went to the net behind every serve, first and second deliveries in upsetting ninth-seeded Juan Carlos Ferrero, 6-3, 7-5, 7-6. The Spaniard hardly ventured to the net at all.

Compared with the victories by fellow lucky loser, George Bastl over Pete Sampras, the stunning display by Paradorn Srichaphan and Olivier Rochus's defeat of Marat Safin, this was small fry. After all Ferrero, who was runner-up at the French Open, was still an apprentice on grass although he deserved

ro • hewitt v carraz

Right: Gregory Carraz.

Bottom left: Tim Henman.

Bottom: Scott Draper.

Below right: Lleyton Hewitt.

Top: Amanda Coetzer.

Top right: Jeff Morrison.

Above: Mario Ancic.

Far right: Juan Carlos Ferrero.

Right: Elena Baltacha celebrates her win over Coetzer.

ancic v vacek

credit for at least giving it a go — unlike some notable compatriots. Even though he could probably be forgiven because he was on honeymoon, it did not go unnoticed that Albert Costa, as well as his best man, Alex Corretja, two of the most strident critics who prompted Wimbledon to abandon its old ranking policy, again opted not to compete.

Not that anything could diminish Morrison's excitement. He had only been given his chance, after losing in the qualifying, when Germany's Tommy Haas had to fly to Florida to be with his parents after they had been seriously injured in a road accident.

Morrison acknowledged that the events of the previous day had inspired him. 'When you see guys going onto the big courts and beating seeded players, it makes you realise that you can achieve the same thing,' he said. It did not take him long to impress the crowd. It was a new experience for him and he was determined to enjoy it. He not only hammered down big serves but also went for his volleys and overheads with equal strength and gusto. Above all, he won over the crowd with his big smile, not just after he hit winners but even on the few occasions he made a hash of things, such as when he almost slam-dunked an overhead yards wide when serving for the second set.

Despite Ferrero having an early mini-break and leading 4-1 in the tie-break, a careless backhand pulled Morrison back to 4-4. Then, having been granted another lifeline when enthusiasm got the better of the American rookie as he double faulted on his first match point, Ferrero's wanton forehand over the baseline on the second match point showed how much he still has to learn about playing on grass.

Mario Ancic, the first of the tournament's giant-killers when he knocked out Roger Federer, slipped back into obscurity, at least for the time being. With the serve, which maintained such a high level of penetration and control two days earlier, lacking consistency, he was comprehensively beaten by Jan Vacek of the Czech Republic, 6-4, 6-4, 7-5. Ancic then created more impact than he had done in the match by telling Bob Brett he no longer wanted him to remain his coach. 'He told me that he was not happy with the way I suggested he prepared for the French Open and my attention was divided because I also have a tennis camp in Paris' Brett said.

Jarkko Nieminen's Wimbledon also came to an end when he was beaten 6-3, 6-4, 6-3 by 28-year-old Austrian, Julian Knowle.

The ladies' game in Britain was given a much-needed boost by Baltacha's fine 5-7, 6-4, 6-2 victory over Coetzer, even though the South African no longer has the tenacity or the speed which once lifted her to third in the world rankings. 'People were going bananas, it was brilliant. My hair was standing on the back of my neck I had so much fun' said Baltacha in her inescapable Scottish accent after her triumph on an overflowing No. 3 Court which ended with a huge roar from the crowd and Baltacha's mother kissing her daughter's coach.

The turning point came when Baltacha, angered by a line call, broke for 3-2 in the second set after a game of several deuces. From then on she began hitting her serves and forehands with additional power and confidence. More importantly she was also following her serves into the net with increasing frequency in the final set, something she had

Monica Seles (left) at full stretch as she moved into the third round, but no matter how swiftly she covered the court, Virginia Ruano Pascual (right) could not resist the Venus Williams power.

Far right: the evening sun sets on Court 6 as the women's doubles event gets under way.

always been reluctant to do.

Otherwise the main news of the day in the ladies' singles was the latest setback for Kim Clijsters as she became the principal casualty of the day. The world number five had been trying to mask the impact of her persistent shoulder problem but was unable to do so as she slipped to a 7-6, 6-2 defeat by Elena Likhovtseva. An operation to remedy the problem had been discussed but for the moment she settled simply for being able to give maximum court-side support for her boyfriend, Lleyton Hewitt.

She refused to accept that the shoulder was the root cause of her defeat. 'I just played an opponent who was better than me and made few unforced errors' she said. 'I had a lot of chances to break in the first set and even set points. I was also ahead in the tie-break. If you want to win then when you create chances you've got to take them.'

Fellow Belgian, Justine Henin, played with greater pace than in the previous round to overcome Denisa Chladkova, a Czech outside the top 100, 6-2, 7-5, while Venus Williams, the top seed, had little difficulty in overcoming Virginia Ruano Pascual, the previous year's first-round winner over Martina Hingis, 6-3, 6-1.

Henin's next opponent would be Myriam Casanova, 17, the Swiss qualifier who beat the 29th-seeded Austrian, Barbara Schett, while seasoned campaigners, Monica Seles and Conchita Martinez also progressed, the latter at the expense of Switzerland's 17th-seeded Patty Schnyder.

FRIDAY 28 JUNE

day 5

This was the day that supporters of Tim Henman lost their squatting rights on 'The Hill'. Instead this shrine for those without Centre or No. 1 Court seats became the exclusive preserve of the Greg Rusedski fan club as they roared encouragement and waved their flags while watching the television pictures from Centre Court of him overwhelming 13th-seeded Andy Roddick.

In wonderfully aggressive, almost swash-buckling mood, the left-hander thrilled the equally noisy and enthusiastic crowd inside the arena as he swept into the fourth round for the third time in four years with a resounding 6-3, 6-4, 6-2 win which kept alive the tantalising dream that there might even be an all-British Jubilee final.

From the moment he pounced to break Roddick by constantly attacking his serve in the eighth game of the first set, one always felt that Rusedski was on a victory roll. 'I knew I had to come up with a good match today' he said after taking only 85 minutes to complete a victory which prompted former champion, John McEnroe, to say 'Great stuff, Greg; watch out Xavier Malisse' — his challenger in the fourth round.

Roddick often looked bewildered by the sheer pace, tenacity and fire in Rusedski's game. Even before the first set was over, he was looking up at coach Tarik Benhabilies and holding out his hands as if to say 'What on earth can I do with him in this mood?' After completing the opening set with his fifth ace, Rusedski immediately broke once more in the first game of the second. Time after time he pulled Roddick from side to side with his returns or well-placed serves and then fired winners into the space which had been created.

The defeat of 11th-seeded Roddick hard on the heels of Malisse's impressive straight-sets victory over fifth-seeded Russian, Yevgeny Kafelnikov, meant there had been no let-up in the decimation of the seeds. Only three of the top 16 remained — Tim Henman, Lleyton Hewitt and the always-threatening 16th-seeded Frenchman, Nicolas Escude. The added boost for Rusedski as he went home that night, secure in the knowledge that he had reached the second week, was that

Left: No lack of American support for Andy Roddick (below) but Britain's ebullient Greg Rusedski (right) was unmistakeably the master in this match.

It was another good day for the big servers. Mark Philippoussis, shown at the bottom left of the opposite page, kept his fluids topped up on the way to beating Nicolas Kiefer, while Richard Krajicek (left) ended what Paradorn Srichaphan will remember as the best Grand Slam week of his career.

Ecuador's Nicolas Lapentti was the only remaining seed ranked higher than him in his half of the draw.

At the same time, Rusedski knew that Richard Krajicek and Mark Philippoussis, also in his half of the draw and heading for a fourth-round showdown, were showing signs of running into their best form at the right time. Philippoussis became joint leader of the ace table, with fellow Australian, Wayne Arthurs, after pounding down another 33 in his resounding comeback to beat Germany's Nicolas Kiefer, 3-6, 6-3, 6-4, 6-2. It took his ace total from three matches to 81.

Krajicek delivered only 11 in his nevertheless thoroughly emphatic 7-6, 6-4, 6-2 defeat of Paradorn Srichaphan, Andre Agassi's conqueror on what had been 'Black Wednesday' for so many principal names. Even so he was still averaging 20 aces a match.

Ironically after all his various injuries in the past, it was a new problem which forced him to send for the trainer this time. Blood blisters had burst beneath the nails of both his big toes. He wanted the trainer to give him a mild anaesthetic which would have left them numb — but that was not permitted. Instead they were sprayed with ice. 'That didn't really help' said Krajicek, who also talked of 'muscle stiffness' because he had played so few matches — four in 20 months.

Although he lost his serve early in the match, it remained, as ever, one of the key facets of his game, especially in the crucial tie-break, which he took from a mini-break down by breaking for 6-5 with a spectacular forehand cross-court winner. He then rounded off the set with an ace.

Philippoussis put the loss of the first set against Kiefer down to the German 'coming out of the blocks a lot faster than me.' Despite his high tally of aces, the Australian was also aware that there had been an ominous crop of double faults between them. 'I know I've got to cut out the doubles but the good thing is that almost every time I double faulted, I came up with another ace straight away.'

Just when Kafelnikov was probably thinking that he could be a major beneficiary of the seeding carnage all around him, enabling him to make a worthwhile challenge for the first time since he reached the last eight seven years earlier, he was comprehensively beaten by Belgium's Xavier Malisse. 'I could just as easily have been two sets up rather than two sets down' said the Russian, well aware of his failure to take real chances in both of them.

At a time when Malisse was having trouble with his footholds and making too many unforced errors, Kafelnikov rashly overhit two forehands when serving at 3-4 in the tie-break and effectively threw the set away. The second reached a thrilling climax when Malisse, who had trailed 2-4 but broken back to 4-4, more importantly, staved off two break points in holding for 5-4. On the first of those break points there was an incredible rally, admittedly sometimes at half pace, which seemed to go on forever until the stylish Malisse guided a perfect backhand down the line with the 43rd stroke of the point. Thereafter it was all Malisse.

For the second time in his career, Arthurs, the Pinner-based Australian, who trains at Sutton, reached the last 16 at The Championships, without dropping his serve. The 31-year-old left-hander emerged triumphant from a predictably serve-dominated battle with Taylor Dent. Except for mini-breaks in the tie-breaks, neither player lost their serve. It was the first time this has happened at Wimbledon since 1999, when Arthurs was also involved and only the fourth time since tie-breaks were introduced in 1971 that they were needed to decide the outcome of all of the first four sets.

Dent, son of the former Australian Davis Cup player, Phil, earned only one break point in the first three sets and he fought to contain his opponent's clinical volleys and heavy forehands. The score was 7-6, 7-6, 6-7, 7-6 with Dent left to ponder if the score might not have been reversed had he not double faulted twice in succession in the second-set tie-break.

The win by Arthurs was to bring him up against a player that few, other than the South Americans, had been following too closely thus far — David Nalbandian, seeded 28 but a first-time visitor from Argentina. On this particular day he had ended the giant-killing exploits

All smiles (right) from Xavier Malisse after he upset a weary Yevgeny Kafelnikov (far right).

Bottom right: Wayne Arthurs in familiar, aggressive mood against fellow big-server Taylor Dent (below).

Below left: David Nalbandian began to make his move by ousting Pete Sampras's conqueror, George Bastl.

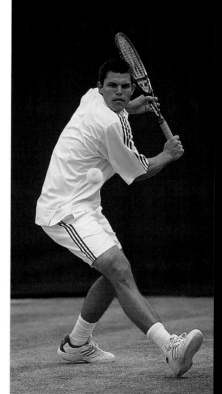

bove: Serena Williams.

ar left: Els Callens.

eft: Daniela Hantuchova.

ight: Jennifer Capriati.

of George Bastl, who had knocked out Pete Sampras, by overwhelming the Swiss player, 6-2, 6-2, 6-2. Even then there was no hint of the headlines Nalbandian would be making a week later.

Olivier Rochus, the last of the trio who had created such a stir on Day Three, along with Srichaphan and Bastl, also came to the end of the road, losing 6-0, 7-5, 6-3 to Arnaud Clement, even though the Frenchman needed extensive treatment to an injured right thigh in the closing stages of the second set.

For a while No. 2 Court looked like claiming another major victim when Els Callens, a Belgian qualifier ranked 119 and with little form to boast about earlier in the year, briefly held the upper hand in both sets against second-seeded Serena Williams. However, her lack of experience at this level, and nervousness on the big points, negated those she had gained from regularly slicing returns low to her opponent's feet and cost her a day in the sun. She was beaten 7-6, 7-6.

Serving for the first set, Callens had allowed her by now almost desperate opponent to break back to love and then in the ensuing tie-break ruined her chance by double faulting twice. Then, having broken to lead 3-2 in the second set and reaching a point for 5-2, she was thwarted as Williams charged across the court to deliver a remarkable, full-stretch lob. 'She was just a bit better than me on the important points' said a disappointed Callens, while Williams, knowing she had not played well, blamed her shoes. 'I kept slipping out there and that made me nervous about moving' she explained.

Jennifer Capriati, generally regarded as having the best hope among any of the other 126 competitors to prevent an all-Williams final, also went a break down at the start against Daja Bedanova but recovered swiftly and effectively enough with her added weight of shot from the back of the court to record a comfortable 6-4, 6-2 victory.

Serena Williams and Capriati were by no means the only ladies who reached the last 16 without dropping a set. Among the others was Williams's next opponent, Chanda Rubin, who followed up her success at Eastbourne the week before and completed an impressive

first Wimbledon week with a 6-4, 6-1 defeat of Tatiana Panova — her second defeat of a seed. Capriati's next challenger, Eleni Daniilidou from Greece, also won more admirers by the way she fended off the more experienced Miriam Oremans.

Jelena Dokic stirred Centre Court passions for a while by squandering nine set points and serving a rash of double faults in the second set before taking change of her match to beat Nathalie Dechy of France, 7-5, 6-2. Daniela Hantuchova, despite 30 unforced errors, served reliably enough to beat the Slovenian, Maja Matevzic 6-4, 6-4. She closed out her win with one of the best shots of the match — a running forehand cross-court struck at full stretch.

Meanwhile French hopes that Mary Pierce would survive the first week and then start feeling confident enough, after her lengthy absence, to lift her game in the second, fell apart when she was beaten 3-6, 6-4, 6-1 by a 134-ranked American, Laura Granville. In contrast to her entrance to No. 3 Court, upright and haughty, she was barely able to mask the mental pain as she left, having lost her temper and her control as the unforced errors mounted in the second and third sets. Not for the first time, her anger had got the better of her.

THE CHAMPIONSHIPS WIMBLEDON

SATURDAY 29 JUNE
day 6

www.wimbledon.org
118 mph
IBM

Once he had known he would be facing Wayne Ferreira for a place in the fourth round, Tim Henman said 'That will mean me stepping up the level a bit.' It was certainly the case, for it was only in the fourth set that the British number one began to impose his authority after often struggling in the first three on his way to a 7-6, 3-6, 7-6, 6-1 victory.

The Centre Court was abuzz with excitement, with more than a fair sprinkling of South African flags helping to brighten up the scene. It soon became clear that the match was going to hinge on whether Henman's re-modelled serve — reduced power in search of greater accuracy and consistency — would stand up in the face of Ferreira's returns.

For most of the first three sets it was a nail-biting dilemma. Ferreira started slowly, slipping to 1-4 before those stunning returns began to find their range and timing. Once they did, Henman soon knew he was facing a dogfight. Although the atmosphere was often more captivating than the tennis in the first set, the three brilliant returns which Ferreira fashioned to break back in the ninth game set the improved tone for what was to follow.

As Henman conceded later, he might easily have lost the first set, as well as the second when his game faltered all too often. He trailed 2-4 in the tie-break and at 6-4 Ferreira reached two set points, but on the first Henman's dipping low return forced a volley into the net, while on the second he slipped and was stranded out of position. To add to Ferreira's woes, after several games during which his backhand had looked a possible match-winner, two backhand blunders then cost him the set which had lasted 1 hour 6 minutes.

The second was all Ferreira and it looked

like staying that way when Henman missed a game point and was broken to 1-2, in what was to be the pivotal third set, by a backhand service return which had just enough top spin to make it drop in at the last second. Henman broke straight back and might have avoided another tie-break, which was to be the subject of so much controversy, but for the brilliant way the South African saved three set points while holding for 5-5.

Henman once again began poorly in the tie-break. Another rasping backhand return sent Ferreira racing to a 4-0 lead but at 4-1, to Ferreira's disbelief and horror, Portuguese umpire, Jorge Dias, an experienced official on the ATP tour, overruled both the side and baseline umpires, on a shot to the corner, which they signalled had been a Ferreira winner. So instead of 5-1, it was 4-2. Ferreira still won the next point to make it 5-2, somewhat diluting the strength of his complaints later that the call alone cost him the set. On the other hand, one could appreciate his dismay.

Henman, who closed the gap with a superb low volley, was grateful for a Ferreira backhand which finished up in the net plus a double fault which gave him the first of the four set points he needed to escape.

Later, after he had wilted meekly in the fourth set, Ferreira vented his anger, not only against Dias but also against Henman, whom he accused of intimidating the official by pointing that the ball was out — a habit which has become all too common in the game these days. Henman said his gut reaction at the time was that the ball was out. 'But that was hope, as much as anything. If it was in, he has every right to complain. If he made a mistake, I can't help that.'

There was tension in the crowd and in one of the staff boxes as Tim Henman (above) took on Wayne Ferreira, especially when the South African expressed his displeasure over a controversial line call with umpire Jorge Diaz.

The match had taken 3 hours 29 minutes and it was another two hours, after Justine Henin had been given a thorough workout by yet another fast-improving Swiss prospect, Myriam Casanova, 6-4, 6-4 — certainly a name to watch for in the future — before Lleyton Hewitt also stepped onto Centre Court. He wasted no time in taking charge against the little-known Austrian, Julian Knowle, producing an awesome display of power and precision as he outclassed his opponent, 6-2, 6-1, 6-3, in 1 hour 28 minutes.

Meanwhile the cull of the lower-order seeds continued. Nicolas Escude, struggling with a strained stomach muscle, was beaten 6-2, 1-6, 6-3, 6-3, by Russia's Mikhail Youzhny and that meant Hewitt and Henman were the only seeds remaining among the top 16, the lowest on record.

The straight-sets defeat of American lucky loser, Jeff Morrison, by 18th-seeded Sjeng Schalken from Holland 6-4, 7-6, 6-0, also meant it was the first time since The Championships moved from Worple Road to Church Road in 1922 that the United States, for so long the dominant nation in men's tennis, had no representative left in the last 16 of the men's singles.

For a while it looked as if the real drama of the day would happen on No. 1 Court. On paper the clash between defending champion, Venus Williams and 31-year-old Maureen Drake from Toronto and ranked a modest 110 in the world, would be little more than a pleasant evening aperitif before everyone went off for dinner.

Wrong! Williams, who had arrived on court with her left knee heavily bandaged, did not win a single point in the first two games as Drake opened up a 3-0 lead. Things appeared to be returning to normal when Venus, still world number one at the time, took the next four games. Williams, though, was still moving gingerly and hitting with strange timidity, by her standards, so when Drake took the first set 7-5, the few empty seats there were rapidly filled.

From then on, however, although Drake continued to enjoy her ready rapport with a crowd that cheered every point she won, Williams threw off caution and quickly stifled

the possibility of what would have been a sensational upset by winning 5-7, 6-2, 6-1.

Drake did not win a point in the second set until the third game when she audaciously lobbed her towering opponent as she was coming to the net. The crowd erupted again — she held her arms aloft and she deserved the prolonged ovation she received at the end, even if the 83 minutes she had kept Williams on court meant merely, for many of them, that dinner had been delayed.

Earlier in the day, the Williams sisters had considered withdrawing from the doubles because of the tendonitis in Venus's left knee, a recurring problem. After physiotherapy, however, she decided she was fit enough to join Serena even later that evening as they beat Kveta Hrdlickova of the Czech Republic and Patty Schnyder of Switzerland, 6-1, 6-2.

The other most significant ladies' singles matches of the day featured one player just starting out on what British tennis followers will hope is a successful career in major tournaments and a former world number one, who, even in victory, talked sadly that her career might be coming to an end.

Elena Baltacha, the bespectacled 18-year-old British girl, born in the Ukraine but brought up in Ipswich and Scotland, where her father pursued his career as a professional footballer, demonstrated a spirit and promise which delighted the crowd on No. 2 Court. After she had eventually lost 6-4, 7-6 to Russia's 48th-ranked Elena Likhovtseva, whose previous scalp had come from Kim Clijsters, Baltacha's coach, Alan Jones, summed it up by saying 'Bally is still extremely green behind the ears in certain aspects of the game but the last week has been a crucial learning curve. Likhovtseva knows all the tricks and she used them in a way any experienced player would against a girl new to this sort of thing. There were mind games going on out there.'

He was referring to the way Likhovtseva arrived on court nine minutes after Baltacha and then only after a telephone call to the referee's office. Then at the end of the first set, as if to repay her opponent for taking a toilet break after the warm-up, she decided to answer the call of nature 40 minutes later. If

Top: Lleyton Hewitt.

Above: Julian Knowle.

Above right: Venus Williams.

Right: Justine Henin.

Centre right: Myriam Casanova.

Far right: Maureen Drake.

Ken Rosewall (left) acknowledges the cheers from the crowd on Middle Saturday when leading personalities from the world of sport were guests in the Royal Box.

Bottom left: Another favourite from days gone by, Martina Navratilova, showed that even at 45 she was fit and competitive in the doubles.

Likhovtseva's stalling tactics were designed to distract Baltacha, such as turning her back when she was ready to serve, they worked for the teenager saw a 4-1 second-set lead slip from her grasp and, most disappointing of all, she failed to win even one point when she was serving in the tie-break.

Monica Seles, who has never quite looked the same since that horrific incident in Hamburg in May 1993 when an intruder ran onto court during a WTA event and stabbed her between the shoulder blades, found the form she needed just in time to overcome the supremely athletic Ai Sugiyama from Japan, 4-6, 6-1, 6-4. Yet the popular Seles, who had won eight of the previous nine Grand Slam tournaments in which she had played and been runner-up at Wimbledon when the attack took place, hinted that her playing days may be numbered.

'I think I'm going to take a year off and just have a life, you know' she said 'just enjoying time with my friends and family at home without a schedule. Since I was seven or eight, I've always been keeping to a schedule. I see an end to my professional career. I will keep playing so long as I can because I love it as a sport but when the point comes that I am tired mentally or bodily, I'll stop and enjoy a little bit of life.'

Opposite: Monica Seles was determined as ever against Ai Sugiyama.

Below: The All England Club Chairman Tim Phillips presents Robert Brooke, Chairman of the Dunlop Slazenger Group, with a Waterford crystal bowl to celebrate Slazenger's 100 years as official supplier of tennis balls to The Championships.

Above left: Tim Henman.

Far left: Michel Kratochvil.

Left: Greg Rusedski.

Above: Xavier Malisse.

At 8 pm, during later stages of the gripping matches involving Tim Henman v. Michel Kratochvil and Greg Rusedski v. Xavier Malisse, more than 13.3 million were tuned in to BBC1, the highest figure for five years.

While Lleyton Hewitt moved inexorably towards justifying his status on top of the world rankings and the Williams sisters stepped up the heat in the ladies' singles, there was another nail-biting afternoon for Tim Henman as he survived a torrid five-set battle on No. 1 Court.

'I really don't understand how I won that match' the British number one said after he had fended off Switzerland's Michel Kratochvil 7-6, 6-7, 4-6, 6-3, 6-2 to reach the quarter finals for the sixth time in his ninth Wimbledon.

He celebrated his success with rather more relief than excitement. 'At two sets to one down and 1-2 in the fourth, I was out of there but the good old crowd got me going again' he said. 'I was fighting for every point and it's amazing what you can do, even when you're not playing your best. If I keep winning it really doesn't matter how I play. If I'm still alive, that's the most important thing.

'At times I'm sure it wasn't pleasant to watch and it certainly wasn't great to play but I'll take a lot of confidence from the way I played. It was probably quite exciting to watch but too exciting to play in.'

Henman twice sent for the trainer because of a stomach upset, initially just before they went off for rain and, at one stage, was given smelling salts. 'During the delay, though, I felt more and more tired. From 4-1 up I lost seven out of eight games and it certainly wasn't looking pretty. It was purely my determination and my feelings for this tournament that pulled me through.'

There were 4 hours 13 minutes on the clock when Kratochvil's final service return ended up in the net and Henman was able to look towards the heavens, offering thanks for his success. As he said, he had not been impressive. He was lucky not to have lost the first set, for his opponent effectively handed it to him by delivering three of his 17 undermining double faults when he was serving for a 5-4 lead.

Henman could also look back with concern on the way 15 of the 22 break points he created, or was offered, slipped away. The conditions did not help. 'They were the most difficult I've played in here' he explained. 'Once the sun went down and we were playing in the shade, it felt very heavy and the conditions were pretty slow. It was also pretty windy, so blustery that it made every shot difficult.'

Kratochvil will certainly regard this as a match he could have won. His ferocious forehands as well as a handful of brilliant lobs meant he was a constant threat. Yet in addition to those nervous three double faults when the opening set looked to be going into his pocket, another, which gave Henman the break back to 1-2 in the fifth, was equally damaging.

The tension throughout was considerable and never more so than in the first four games of the final set which lasted 35 minutes. It could have gone either way and Henman had to save another break point at 2-2 before, on the stroke of four hours, spectacularly breaking again with a rousing forehand cross-court winner.

By then it was already known that Henman's next foe would be the unseeded Brazilian, Andre Sa, one of three South Americans through to the quarter finals of a tournament in which, hitherto, only eight had reached that stage in the 33 years of Open tennis. Sa, inspired by his team's World Cup triumph the day before, had come through 6-3, 7-5, 4-6, 6-3 against the equally unseeded Feliciano Lopez from Spain.

Meanwhile Greg Rusedski's hopes of matching Henman's progress were left in abeyance overnight when bad light forced his fourth-round battle with Belgium's Xavier Malisse to be stopped at 8.53 pm, when they were two sets all. Rusedski had twice been a set up but Malisse was starting to dominate the match with heavy forehands, after saving two break points in two separate games in that important fourth set, when the break came.

The weather interruptions meant that the tantalising contest between Mark Philippoussis and Richard Krajicek was postponed until the following day.

Hewitt reached the last eight as the only man yet to drop a set. He had again been in totally convincing form as he dismissed the promising Russian, Mikhail Youzhny 6-3, 6-3, 7-5 and said 'I haven't lost a lot of energy so far which is a good thing bearing in mind the way I play. I feel confident that I can

Lleyton Hewitt (far left) dealt comfortably with Mikhail Youzhny (left).

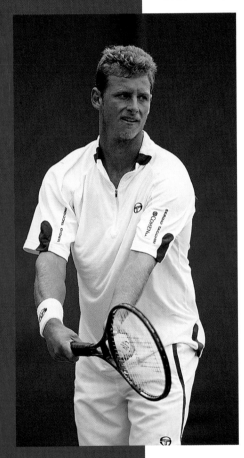

Above: David Nalbandian's stinging service returns at last found a way to break the Wayne Arthurs (left) serve.

still lift my game up another gear and I will probably have to in the next round against [Sjeng] Schalken.'

Schalken, who had kept Hewitt under pressure for long spells before losing to him at both the French Open and Queen's Club in his two previous tournaments, earned his third successive confrontation with the Australian by just serving well enough, often enough, to keep ahead of the Czech, Jan Vacek, 6-2, 7-5, 7-5.

Two dark horses, one, Nicolas Lapentti, well established as a grass-court player, the other a newcomer, David Nalbandian, filled the bottom two places in the last eight draw.

Lapentti, who had won only two matches in five previous visits to The Championships, but had proved Ecuador's Davis Cup match-winner against Britain on No. 1 Court in 2000, squeezed through 3-6, 7-5, 2-6, 7-5, 6-3 against France's Arnaud Clement.

Nalbandian, only the second player from Argentina after Guillermo Vilas in 1976 to make it through to the last eight, suddenly demanded respect and attention when he became the first player to break the formidable serve of Australian left-hander, Wayne Arthurs, to pave the way for an impressive 6-4, 7-6, 2-6, 7-6 victory.

Arthurs, who in his debut year of 1999 registered a sequence of 111 service games, including three in qualifying, without being broken, went into the match with an unblemished record in 54 games but paid heavily for his solitary lapse in the seventh game of their 2 hours 44 minutes match.

Daniela Hantuchova proved that she has considerably more than never-ending legs

Frenchman Arnaud Clement (above) in a typically Gallic gesture as Ecuador's Nicolas Lapentti rallied from two sets to one down to beat him.

Daniela Hantuchova (opposite) won a thrilling fourth-round contest with Jelena Dokic (left) while Elena Likhovtseva (below) proved too consistent for the more experienced Manuela Maleeva (below left).

and a pretty face going for her when she had the last word in a fascinating battle with Jelena Dokic. The Slovakian teenager, who, through no obvious intent on her part, had become a rival for Anna Kournikova in the glamour stakes this year, just edged out the Yugoslavian 6-4, 7-5 in a thrilling match on Court 18.

Hantuchova admitted that she was helped by a rain break of more than two hours just when it looked as if Dokic was on top at 4-2 in the second set and well placed to draw level. 'It's one of the biggest wins of my career — it really means something' said Hantuchova, who is coached by Nigel Sears from Sussex.

Dokic, by contrast, was thoroughly dejected. 'I wasn't happy with the way I played, I didn't move well, made too many errors and was too tight' she suggested, before also insisting that the weather had been a major factor: 'I think I would have won it without the delay. I lost the momentum' she said.

Hantuchova was probably well advised to enjoy the moment, for next up for her would be Serena Williams, who had been six points from victory when the first rain of The Championships sent the players scurrying for cover at 4.37 pm. She required only nine minutes when they resumed to complete her 6-3, 6-3 victory over Chanda Rubin.

At least Rubin fared a little better than fellow American, Lisa Raymond, who was brushed aside 6-1, 6-2 in just 47 minutes by Venus Williams, who would next meet Elena Likhovtseva, a 6-3, 6-4 winner over Magdalena Maleeva.

Justine Henin had to work harder than either of the Williams sisters. She was taken to two tie-breaks, the second of them full of thrilling rallies, before dismissing the 12th-seeded Russian, Elena Dementieva. It earned the Belgian a quarter final against Monica Seles. She proved too strong and too astute for Thailand's Tamarine Tanasugarn who, though ranked 24 in the world, had not taken a set from her in five meetings. Seles won a one-sided match 6-2, 6-2, as did Amelie Mauresmo against the young American qualifier, Laura Granville.

Jennifer Capriati was given a late night

fright by Eleni Daniilidou from Greece for, after running away with the first set, she looked more than content when bad light forced an overnight delay with the scoreboard blinking in near darkness 6-1, 3-6.

Earlier the junior singles had also been underway, providing two stimulating first-round achievements for British players, Alice Barnes and Alex Bogdanovic. Barnes, who had needed to win her way through qualifying as she did not have a world junior ranking, eliminated Su-Wei Hsieh, the top seed from Chinese Taipei 6-4, 6-3.

The Cambridge-based 18-year-old had quit the LTA squad in which she had been working with Davis Cup captain, Roger Taylor, while waiting to take up her place at Stanford University in the United States in September.

Bogdanovic's challenge to become the first British boys' singles champion since Stanley Matthews Junior 40 years earlier began in flawless fashion when he overwhelmed Artem Sitak of Russia 6-0, 6-0 in a mere 35 minutes. Both British prospects were well aware, though, that there were tougher tests ahead.

THE CHAMPIONSHIPS WIMBLEDON

TUESDAY 2 JULY

day 8

Greg Rusedski's hopes were brought down to earth for another year by Belgium's aggressively stylish Xavier Malisse (opposite).

Play was delayed for two hours at the start of Day Eight by rain and ended equally ahead of time when the 'prolonged period of inclement weather', which the weather men had promised would follow the showers, sadly arrived on time.

In between, there were two patches of blue sky to accompany convincing performances by Venus Williams and Justine Henin as they moved into the quarter finals of the ladies' singles. From the British point of view, however, there was a sombre mood, as grey as the skies above, when Greg Rusedski failed to join Tim Henman in the last eight of the men's singles.

Rusedski had what could have been the advantage of serving first in the fifth set which remained to be played after the overnight interruption. It did not work out that way — though it might have done.

Twice in the sixth game, by which time neither serve had been threatened, he reached deuce on the Malisse serve but missed his next service return, allowing the 22-year-old Belgian to escape. Worse still, Rusedski promptly lost his own serve in the game that followed. After failing to put away three volleys on the first point, Rusedski was passed to 0-15, a perfect Malisse lob made it 15-30, and a passing forehand winner accompanied by a roar and the pumped fist took it to 30-40 when the service return was volleyed wide.

'It just came down to one missed volley on the break point and then a forehand up the line which missed by inches' said Rusedski after his 3-6, 6-3, 3-6, 6-3, 6-4 defeat. 'I thought I played the better tennis over the five sets but I just couldn't win the important points.' One of those big moments came when the left-hander had a chance to break back to 5-5 but Malisse, whose clever variation of pace and angles on his serves had been a feature of his play, responded with a perfectly timed ace. Then, after winning a rally of 28 strokes to reach his second match point, he rounded things off with another service winner.

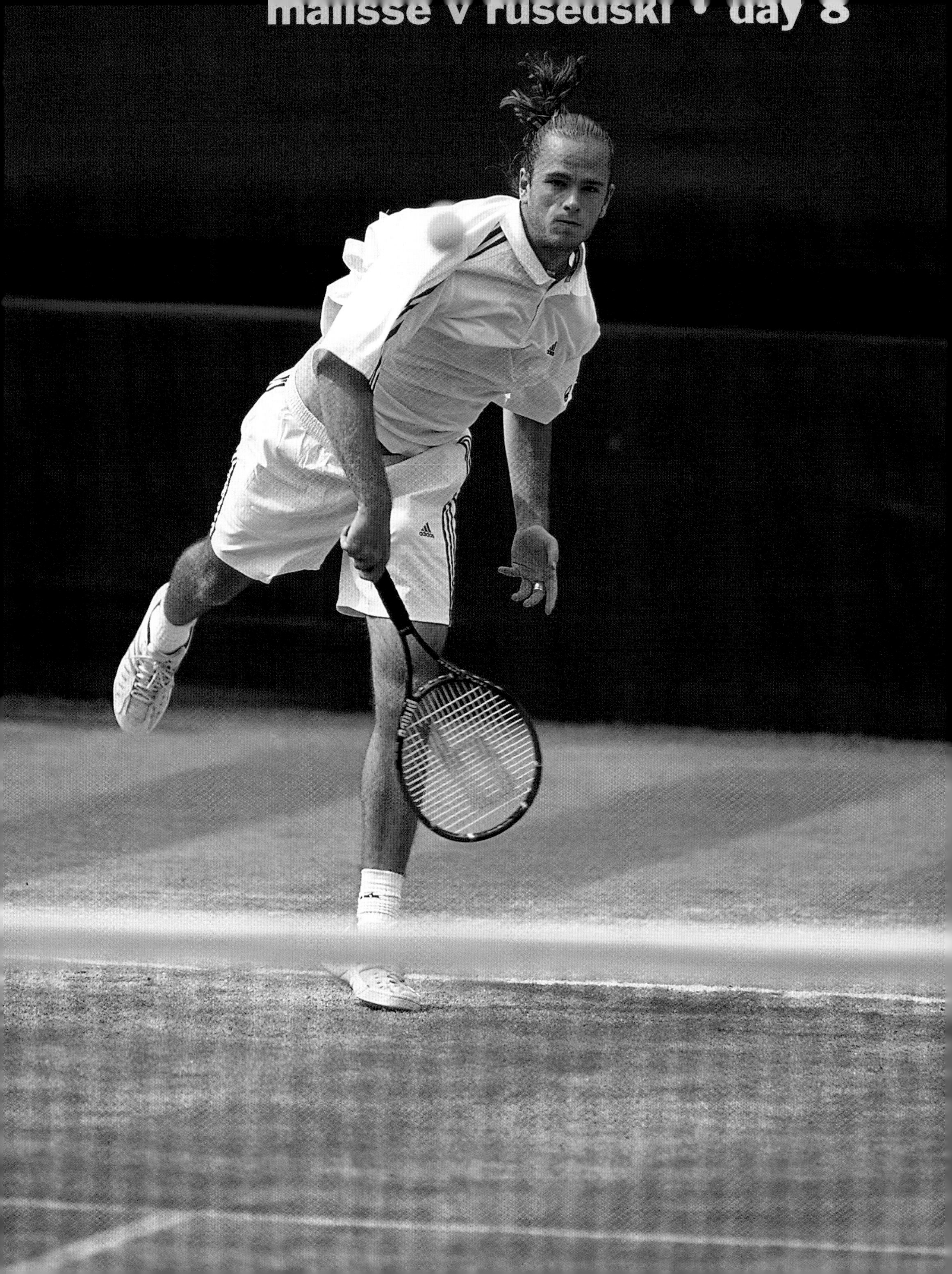

Mark Philippoussis (above) in action against Richard Krajicek (right) who also needed treatment from trainer Bill Norris.

Rusedski, three months away from his 29th birthday, promised 'I'll be back next year. I'm still young so I've still got a few more years left in me to do well. I'm just going to have to come back next year and take my chances' he added, eager to mask that finding a permanent cure to the back problems which had so limited his activity in the first six months of the year might prove to be as important as his form.

Meanwhile Richard Krajicek and Mark Philippoussis were heavily committed to trying to settle a match that had not even started when it should have been decided the day before. They failed. The clash which one Australian writer kept referring to as 'the battle of the crocks' was still unresolved at two tie-breaks all when the weather forced another overnight delay after they had spent three and a half hours pounding thunderous serves, lightning volleys and heavy-duty forehands at one another.

It started 70 minutes late because of the rain but, with neither of the men moving swiftly between rapid-fire points, there was little prospect of them making up for lost time. Krajicek also took a lengthy injury time-out in the second set for treatment to his hamstrings.

Philippoussis took the opening set and clearly should have also taken the second for, when serving for it, he double faulted at 30-30 and then tried, without success, to volley a ball that was going out. The tennis was ferocious but hardly compelling because of the lack of any light and shade. Only six rallies lasted more than four strokes in the first two sets and the pattern rarely changed in the two that followed.

Following the late interruption the previous day of Jennifer Capriati's fourth-round struggle with Eleni Daniilidou, when they were one set all, they faced another long wait, thanks to the weather, before they could resume. It was shortly after 6 pm that they restarted on Court 18 where Capriati only once demonstrated any further sign of the nervousness which had marked her play in the second set the night before. That was at 3-1 when her opponent's backhand twice struck when Capriati least expected it and, under the

Jennifer Capriati (left) rapidly achieved success in her delayed fourth-round match against Eleni Daniilidou. Justine Henin (below) scored one of her best wins of the year by beating Monica Seles (right).

pressure, she twice double faulted. Indeed she had to save three break points before holding with a couple of reassuring baseline winners which sped her to a 6-1, 3-6, 6-1 victory. Her quarter final against Amelie Mauresmo and that of Serena Williams v. Daniela Hantuchova, in the same half of the draw, were scheduled for the following day.

Despite being abbreviated, the day's action in the ladies' singles was still compelling. Justine Henin, the petite Belgian, who possessed deceptive power on both flanks, achieved what she considered to be her finest victory since upsetting Capriati at Wimbledon a year earlier, when she beat Monica Seles 7-5, 7-6.

Seles, the fourth seed, had been in sturdy form in earlier rounds. She also went into the match with a 4-0 record against Henin but was unable to thwart her opponent's extra pace about the court and her all-round versatility and vitality. Delighted though Henin was with her triumph, it was not a good day for Seles. There were too many lapses of concentration. Although recovering from 2-4 to make a fight of the first set at 5-4, she then dropped the next three games, losing the set with a forehand error off a ball which in earlier years would have given her no trouble. She also led 4-1 in the second set before the errors started creeping in again and allowing Henin to finish with a flourish.

When Venus Williams blew away the Russian, Elena Likhovtseva, 6-2, 6-0 in 47 minutes, her total time on court in reaching the quarter finals for a fifth time amounted to 3 hours 53 minutes — less than the length of Tim Henman's fourth-round match against Michel Kratochvil the day before.

Such was her commanding authority over an opponent who had already upset fifth-seeded Kim Clijsters and 19th-seeded Magdalena Maleeva that she took only 27 minutes over the first set and 20 to win the second, during which she lost only seven points. Yet she was far from satisfied.

'Nowadays I expect myself to be almost perfect' she said. 'I'd like to improve a lot more. I think I hit too many balls down the middle and maybe my preparation was a little slow. I'll be studying myself before the next match [against Henin] with a view to keeping down my unforced error account.'

In the handful of doubles matches which managed to get on court, Don Johnson and Jared Palmer reached the semi-finals in defence of their men's doubles title with a 7-6, 6-4, 6-4 victory over the Czech partnership of Martin Damm and the veteran Cyril Suk, but stepping up the pace also were Jonas Bjorkman and Todd Woodbridge as they dismissed Mahesh Bhupathi of India and Max Mirnyi of Belarus, 6-2, 6-3, 6-4.

For much of this day, the court coverers worked harder than many of the players. Because of the lengthy rain delays the day before, the proposed start had been brought forward to 12 noon on all courts but the frustratingly persistent light drizzle meant that it was 3.55 pm before the first matches were underway. Between then and 7.50 pm, when another sharp shower sent everyone in search of cover once more, including Tim Henman, who had just taken the first set of his quarter final from Brazil's Andre Sa, there was no lack of action — or anxiety, especially in the referee's office, as the backlog of matches rose to more than 130. In some respects, though, the real drama of the day was still to come. While most players, Henman and Sa among them, were sent home for the night, Richard Krajicek and Mark Philippoussis had been told to wait in the hope that there might still be a long enough window in the clouds for them to complete their fourth-round singles match that was then running two days behind schedule.

Without that match finishing, it would have been impossible to complete the quarter finals, even a day late, on Day Ten. That, in turn, would have had the knock-on effect of upsetting plans to stage both semi-finals on schedule.

The fingers-crossed optimism of the officials was rewarded. By 8.50 pm Krajicek and Philippoussis resumed combat on No. 1 Court and 21 minutes later, amid noisy and enthusiastic support for both players, the 1996 champion from Holland struck the last of his feast of unreturnable serves to deny the Australian a fourth successive appearance in the last eight.

A smiling Krajicek admitted that he had expected to be with his wife and their two children in their holiday home in Majorca by the middle of Wimbledon's second week, instead of looking forward to a quarter final against Xavier Malisse. 'This is unbelievable, something I could never have expected,' he said.

One double fault, which cost Philippoussis the first game of the much-delayed final set, effectively settled the serve-dominated match. 'I fought as hard as I could and that's my only regret' said the grimly disappointed loser, who

The grounds staff were kept busy as the rain heavily interrupted play on Day 9 but the patient crowd was rewarded by a thrilling late-night victory for an overjoyed Richard Krajicek (right) against Mark Philippoussis.

had looked poised for victory 24 hours earlier when he had two chances to break for a 6-5 lead in the fourth set, when he was leading by two sets to one.

Philippoussis actually won the most points, 201 to Krajicek's 188. He also struck three more aces, 27 to 24, and re-iterated his belief that 'I will win this tournament one day.' On the other hand, Krajicek produced more of the biggest shots on the most important points and though he was twice 0-30 on serve during the nail-biting final few games, he was always able to serve his way out of trouble. It had been an amazing nine days for someone who barely a month earlier had been giving serious thought to the idea of re-tiring from tennis.

While Krajicek celebrated, it had been a day of growing despair for many players as they waited to see if and when they would be able to play. It was after 6 pm when Henman eventually started against Sa and then it was interrupted for another hour before being ter-minated again by the weather moments after he had taken the first set, 6-3.

Expecting delays when he first arrived at the All England Club that morning, Henman said 'I don't care how long it takes, so long as I win.' After his semi-final against Goran Ivanise-vic the previous year which spanned three days, he was used to waiting, even though, as he added, 'It doesn't get any easier.'

There was concern about Henman's fitness but Bill Norris, the ATP tour trainer, who had twice treated him for a stomach upset 48 hours earlier, suggested that stress might also have played its part in the player feeling tired and lethargic and that there was no need to fret.

Maybe, but there was still initial concern. Although Sa lost the first two points of a match which began in such bleak light that flashlights from cameras lit the upper reaches of the stands, he not only held for 1-0 but had a break point in the second game before Henman escaped with a service winner, and delivered another to hold the advantage be-fore the rain drove them off for 61 minutes.

It was an altogether more confident Hen-man who returned for the second chapter. Having safely taken the point still required to make it 1-1, he broke for 2-1 at the third

attempt with a strident forehand winner down the line. A further break in the eighth game at least enabled him to have one set in the bag by the time the rain returned and that was it for their day.

On any other day, the big story would have been the way Amelie Mauresmo de-stroyed Jennifer Capriati's dream of being able to shatter almost universal forecasts of an all-Williams final. The American holder of the Australian Open title had been among those most affected by the rain of recent days, all of which seemed to leave her men-tally in arrears of the stylish Mauresmo who had taken advantage of two full days to pre-pare for what became her best performance on grass. The French player, despite reaching the semi-finals of the Australian Open in 1999, remained an under-achiever but sud-denly the lack of self-belief wafted away. She produced a wonderful display of resilient and sustained heavily hit winners to prevent Capriati from reaching the semi-finals for the first time in seven Grand Slams.

Capriati's mental fatigue was demon-strated when she made an unexpected and costly error of judgement seconds before the first rain delay to a match which involved only 60 minutes of action, even though it took al-most six hours to complete. Serving at 2-3, she double faulted to give Mauresmo a break point. Light drizzle was falling and she looked at the umpire, clearly hoping that they would stop, but when no signal was forthcoming she compounded the mistake by double faulting again to give her opponent the psychologically important first service break.

'I probably should have stopped after the first double and could have done' said Capriati, who also had two spells of attention from the trainer as the match ran away from her, 6-3, 6-2. 'I'm not used to playing so aggressively as this but grass gives me the opportunity so it's the obvious thing to do' said Mauresmo, who had gone to the net at every opportunity and put away 17 of her 20 volleying chances to maintain her supremacy over an increasingly despondent opponent.

If Capriati felt irritated by the weather then Daniela Hantuchova and Serena Williams had even more reason to be. Twice they arrived on

Tim Henman (below) and Andre Sa (bottom) were sent home for the nig because of rain after only one set of their quarter final.

Jennifer Capriati battled on after treatment but could not resist the superior power happily delivered by Amelie Mauresmo (far right).

Opposite: The view across Courts 3, 4 and 5 with the new Clubhouse and Millennium Building in the background.

Below left: Martina Navratilova continued her mixed doubles bid with Todd Woodbridge.

Daniela Hantuchova serves (left) but Serena Williams (below) stayed in command, while Britain's Alice Barnes (bottom) reached the last 16 of the girls' singles.

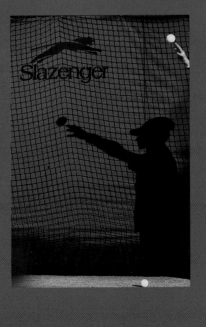

court, warmed up and then had to race off again because it started to rain. On the second occasion, Serena found herself surrounded by grounds staff racing to pull the covers across while she was in the process of hitting a practice forehand over a net which disappeared before Hantuchova had time to make a return.

At the third attempt they completed a set and four games and, in the fourth, Williams tightened the noose to finish with a 6-3, 6-2 victory. Hantuchova, the 11th seed, nevertheless emerged with credit. She refused to be intimidated early on, rallying well and deservedly holding her own for the first seven games, even though there was a nagging belief that it would only be a matter of time before her whipped forehands and double-handed backhands would be tamed by her opponent's awesome power.

The key was a superb lob which Hantuchova opted for on a break point at 3-2. Williams slipped and was mightily relieved as she looked back and saw the ball drop a few inches out, while she remained stranded. The Slovakian, who then lost her serve, had another chance to embarrass the younger Williams sister with a break-back chance at 3-4 but the second seed unleashed a winning serve which was as emphatic as the grunt which went with it and thereafter remained in control.

Elsewhere, between the showers, Martina Navratilova's hopes of becoming the oldest Wimbledon champion in any of the five principal events was thwarted when the 45-year-old, partnered by Todd Woodbridge, went out in the second round of the mixed doubles, 3-6, 6-4, 6-2 to Jonas Bjorkman and Anna Kournikova.

Among the juniors, Alice Barnes reached the last 16 of the girls' singles by beating the American, Shadisha Robinson 6-1, 6-3 and then explained why she was quitting British tennis for Stanford University in America. 'The LTA system doesn't work' claimed Barnes, the only survivor to the third round from the nine British players who began. 'It's best described as a conveyor belt with people dropping off into the reject box — and that's where I was heading.'

A happy Tim Henman (far left) acknowledges the cheers from his supporters (bottom) after his victory over Andre Sa (below) while Lleyton Hewitt (left) was given a huge fright by Holland's Sjeng Schalken, despite the Dutchman's problem with blisters.

Not even the appearance of Venus and Serena Williams, in successive matches on Centre Court in their semi-finals of the ladies' singles, could upstage the unfinished business from the day before in the men's singles, especially the completion of Tim Henman's quarter final with Andre Sa.

Despite play starting two hours earlier than would normally have been the case on Day Ten, Centre Court was well filled by the time the British player, one set to the good overnight, began to take the crowd on another emotional roller-coaster before he once again finished well enough to win 6-3, 5-7, 6-4, 6-3.

Although Sa's experience on grass was limited — there are only three known grass courts in Rio and all are privately owned — he certainly did not play like a grass-court novice, supporting a challenging serve with fine sharp volleys and, as one would expect, secure, penetrating groundstrokes.

During the first two sets of this second session, in which he made little impact on Sa's serve, Henman teased and tormented the feelings of a Centre Court crowd desperate to lift him. Although by winning he stood one match away from the final for the fourth time in five years, he also acknowledged that he would have to play consistently better to take that elusive, extra step.

The first break point of the second set was created by Sa, in the ninth game, and it sparked off a series of games during which both men had their opportunities. Henman actually had two set points at 5-4 but missed the first when he slipped as he tried to cover a backhand pass down the line. On the second Sa hit a winning serve and then capitalised on his survival by adopting all-out attack in the eleventh game. First he hit a screaming backhand winner down the line to 0-15, next a measly 83 mph serve from Henman was returned in similar, dismissive fashion. Then at 30-40 Henman overhit a forehand, giving Sa the chance to serve out and level the match which he did with an almost ominous authority.

Henman's body language was certainly not encouraging at the start of the third set and he was a shade fortunate that, having lost his opening service game, he was able to break back in the second. The tension remained more gripping than most of the tennis, with Henman failing to convert five more break points until he eventually halted the waste to take the set in the tenth game.

Sharp reflexes at the net enabled Henman to put away a vital volley for 15-30 and he then punished Sa for his impudence by passing him comfortably when the Brazilian came in behind his return, 15-40. Although the Oxfordshire player missed with an attempted backhand pass on the first set point, he gave the crowd a resilient taste of what they had been waiting for with a reaching, forehand volley winner on the second.

From then on it was relatively plain sailing for Henman. He broke for 2-0 with a delightful forehand cross-court dink volley and held on to the advantage until completing his win after 3 hours 10 minutes with a first volley in support of his serve on his second match point.

It was not until almost an hour after he was safely through to the semi-finals that Henman knew, as everyone had predicted, that top-seeded Lleyton Hewitt would be the man blocking his path to the final.

Even so, Hewitt, hitherto the only player among the last eight not to have dropped a set, had lost some of his air of invincibility by missing four match points in the third set against Sjeng Schalken and ultimately being a shade lucky to win 6-2, 6-2, 6-7, 1-6, 7-5 on No. 1 Court.

After a routine start between two men who, despite both having match-winning serves, are happiest on the baseline, it became the most thrilling match of The Championships, warranting its three minutes' standing ovation.

Hewitt, despite wasting a host of break points in the third set — 11 during a run of 16 consecutive break-point failures — still looked home and dry when he reached 15-40 on the Schalken serve and then had two more match points when he was leading 6-5. Yet suddenly, he visibly tightened. He started overhitting forehands, a weakness which became a regular and worrying occurrence for him and his coach, Jason Stoltenberg, throughout the rest of the match. Forehand errors cost him the first match point before he netted forehands on the second and third.

Schalken saved the fourth with a snappy backhand volley to end a rally.

The feisty Australian was upset by an overrule which would have pulled him back to 4-4 in the third-set tie-break he was to surrender 7-5, and thereafter it was the tall, upright Dutchman who had more of the key chances but somehow lacked the conviction — and occasionally the luck — to make them count.

Schalken broke twice in the final set but on both occasions failed to build on the opportunity. He also had a break point in the 11th game that would have left him serving for the match but went wide with his attempted forehand down the line after Hewitt had presented him with a huge gap to go for a cross-court winner.

Hewitt, who reached his fifth match point with a brilliant running forehand down the line, fell on his back in a gesture of relief and delight when his success was complete. Yet within minutes the mind games, ahead of the next day's much-hyped clash with Henman, began. Henman supporters were insisting that their man, seeded and ranked below Hewitt, had nothing to lose and all the pressure would be on his rival. Hewitt, through to his first Wimbledon semi-final, saw it differently. 'I'm 21, I'm sure I'm going to have other chances to do well here' he said. 'Obviously for him he's got fewer chances in the future, so there's more pressure on him.'

The stage had been set.

In the other half of the draw, urgent reference to player profiles had unexpectedly become necessary. Most were reasonably acquainted with Xavier Malisse, who followed up his defeat of Greg Rusedski by also ruining the fairytale revival by Richard Krajicek. After all, he had twice beaten Henman at Grand Slams and for a while was working with Henman's former coach, David Felgate.

David Nalbandian, though, was a different matter. His CV, which became a matter of significance after he prevailed in a marathon contest with Nicolas Lapentti, had remained under wraps, even though he had made sufficient progress during the year to be seeded 28. With none of the five grass courts in Rio available for him to prepare he had been fortunate enough to practise on the Hurlingham Club's cricket ground in Rio. Suddenly, though, one remembered that his unheralded ability to play well on the surface, and become Argentina's first Wimbledon semi-finalist, was not exactly a novelty.

Three years earlier he had not only reached the semi-finals of the boys' singles — only to be defaulted for misunderstanding the time of the match and arriving too late — but also won the boys' doubles. This time, still haunted by the experience of being thrown out of the singles, he set his alarm an hour early.

Nalbandian, who had yet to make an appearance on Centre Court, went through agonies on his way into the history books. Looking comfortably in control when he led by two sets and a break, he was still pushed all the way by Lapentti who had taken five sets to win three of his previous four contests. Lapentti continued to threaten even when two breaks down at 1-4 in the final set and rescued one of them, before his opponent finally put away a smash on match point and fell to his knees in joy, winning 6-4, 6-4, 4-6, 4-6, 6-4.

He said he was 'black and blue' from pinching himself to believe what was happening to him. The day had started in muted fashion. Because of the rain-affected schedule, the match was listed on No. 2 Court where only a handful of spectators, apart from a group of Ecuadoran cheerleaders, were present when a fine match began to unfold. By the fifth set it was almost full, with rousing support for both men and especially for the 20-year-old man from Cordoba, who the crowds were beginning to adore. He was already convincing them that he could make further history by reaching the final at his first attempt, bettering John McEnroe's debut run to the semi-finals in 1977.

The fans appreciated his tennis and his sense of humour. 'I think I'll sleep here tonight just to make sure I'm in time to play Malisse' he said.

As for Malisse, he took 2 hours 27 minutes to eliminate an inevitably weary Krajicek, held together by bandages, 6-1, 4-6, 6-2, 3-6, 9-7. He ran away with the first set

Justine Henin's solid
groundstrokes (above) were
still not good enough to
disturb Venus Williams, while
Amelie Mauresmo (top right)
made little impact either
against Serena Williams.

in 20 minutes, frequently ripping winners from all corners of the court but Krajicek's big-hearted defiance twice enabled him to draw level and play a full part in a memorable final set before his 12th double fault gave Malisse the break for 8-7, and he served out for the match.

If anyone remotely questioned the supremacy of Venus and Serena Williams in the ladies' singles, such doubts were surely dispelled when they dropped only eight games between them in their respective semi-final victories over Justine Henin and Amelie Mauresmo.

When Henin broke in Venus's serve in the opening game and then led 2-0 in the first set, there was just a flicker of hope that the defending champion might be seriously stretched. It was not to be, for that was effectively the limit of the Belgian's success in the face of her opponent's hard-hitting efficiency.

Although there was much to admire in the storming way both Williams girls set about their task, there was also a depressing inevitability about the outcome of both matches. One should stress, though, that the blame lay not with them but with the other players, unable to match them. Serena's display as she demolished the French girl who had upset Jennifer Capriati in such impressive, attacking style, was almost faultless. Only once did she allow Mauresmo more than one point on her service games and that was during an extraordinary few minutes early in the second set when she offered her opponent four break points. None were taken and for the rest of the time Mauresmo was simply blown away 6-2, 6-1 by the 20-year-old American, who, by reaching the final, was guaranteed to overtake her sister at the top of the world rankings.

Away from the more serious business of the singles, Venus and Serena returned to court and reached the quarter finals of the ladies' doubles with a 6-2, 6-2 win over Nalbandian's compatriot, Laura Montalvo and Elena Tatarkova of the Ukraine, but the defending champions, American, Lisa Raymond and Australian, Rennae Stubbs, lost the initiative and bowed out 1-6, 7-5, 6-4 in the quarter finals to the Russia-United States combination of Anna Kournikova and Chanda Rubin.

The Williams sisters, Venus (left) and Serena celebrate reaching the semi-finals of the ladies' doubles.

No wonder Australian Ryan Henry (above left) looked so happy after beating Frenchman Clement Morel (above) in the junior boys' singles... the scoreboard reveals the epic scoreline.

Despite her bitter disappointment in the singles, Kournikova also reached the quarter-finals of the mixed doubles. She and Jonas Bjorkman, already through to the semi-finals of the men's doubles, knocked out the Australians, Andrew Kratzmann and Trudi Musgrave 7-5, 6-4. It was not a good day for British juniors. Alex Bogdanovic went out in the second round of the boys' singles, David Brewer and Joshua Goodall in the third, and Alice Barnes's useful start to the week came to an end when she was beaten 7-6, 7-5 in the third round by Russia's Linda Smolenakova.

117

THE CHAMPIONSHIPS
WIMBLEDON

FRIDAY 5 JULY

day 11

henman v hewitt • day 11

Lleyton Hewitt (left) was typically in command from the baseline. Tim Henman was constantly thinking of ways to upset the Australian's supremacy as he towelled down at changeovers but even his best efforts were in vain.

The moment had arrived! The semi-final showdown between top-seeded Lleyton Hewitt and fourth-seeded Tim Henman. In British eyes this was the final before the final. For the fourth time in five years, Henman stood one match away from becoming the first home finalist in the men's singles since Bunny Austin in 1938.

Once again, though, it was not to be. Hard though Henman fought and tried to sustain a strategy he believed could help him to at last beat an opponent who had won all five of their previous meetings, it was never enough.

The only consolation for Henman, if there was any for someone who had just missed out after going so close to a place in the final more often than any other British player since World War Two, was that Hewitt had so vividly demonstrated why he is the best player in the world.

As Henman said after his 7-5, 6-1, 7-5 defeat in a match lasting 2 hours 19 minutes 'The better player won today, there was no question about that. It wasn't through any lack of effort. I just wasn't good enough.'

It was a typically honest response and one which did not deserve to be interpreted as a surrender, as was the case in some of the more lurid tabloid headlines the next day. Fortunately, Hewitt, overjoyed to have played his way into a final he had so often reached in his dreams, put it into perspective.

Asked if he thought Henman's final chance of winning the title had passed him by, he replied 'Whether he can hold up the trophy is another question but he's had an incredible run here in anyone's book. What is it, four semis, a quarter, round of 16 in the last six years? That's a great effort.'

In view of their past record, it was generally felt that Henman's best hope of unsettling an opponent who came into the match un-beaten in 12 meetings on grass would be if he could win the opening set. When he brilliantly broke back from 3-5 to 5-5 playing his best tennis of the fortnight, British spirits rose. Even the Hewitt forehand and first serve showed signs of hiccupping, just as they had done when he lost his way for an even more prolonged time against Sjeng Schalken the day before.

To some extent in giving him such a fright, Schalken had provided a favour. It was soon clear that Hewitt had no intention of allowing his control to slip seriously a second time. In the 11th game the tenacious right-hander from Adelaide, who lobs better than most, provided a brilliant demonstration of that art on the first point as Henman served to try and force a tie-break. A stunning forehand made it 30-0 and then, sandwiching a Henman ace, he struck two of the many wonderful forehand dipping cross-court winners, good enough to break the resolve, as well as the serve, of any opponent.

It did not exactly do the former. Henman defiantly and stubbornly kept striving to find a weakness he could exploit — but there was none. Thereafter, with the first serve in his pocket, Hewitt's game simply fluctuated between being dominant and awesome.

After the events during the first ten days of The Championships, anything was still possible, though only if Henman did everything right and he could somehow become positive and penetrating with his serve and off the ground with relentless consistency. Only then might he force Hewitt into more errors than had become customary.

Despite the frantic urging of the crowd, it never happened. The statistics revealed the true extent of Hewitt's victory. He hit 41 winners to 18 by Henman and made only nine unforced errors against 31 by his opponent.

The rain delay when he was trailing 0-3 in the second set offered Henman one last chance to regroup. Some such interruptions in the past had come to his aid. Others, such as two delays on two successive days when he was close to winning his 2001 semi-final against Goran Ivanisevic, had been disastrous. This time Hewitt resumed firing on all cylinders. He immediately forced two breaks as evidence that, instead of suffering a lull in his form, he was upping it to an even higher level.

He looked unstoppable — at least until he was serving for victory at 5-4 in the third set when, under a fresh burst of all-out attack by Henman, he was forced into three errors and broken to 30. As in the first set, however, Henman was unable to push the closing door back any further. In next to no time he was

15-40 and although saving the first break point, was beaten on the second by a towering, heavily spun lob of stupendous quality.

The British hopes had to be packed away for another year. Hewitt served out for victory to 15-15, rounding things off with an ace and then collapsing on his back on the turf, leaving Henman to say: 'I've given it my best shot. I couldn't have tried any harder.'

He described the defeat as 'the most disappointing' of his four semi-finals losses 'because everyone was thinking that whoever came through in the top half was going to be the favourite for the title. For me to become Wimbledon champion I know I have to improve. It's as simple as that.'

All that was missing for Hewitt at the end of the day was knowing who his rival would be in the final. Xavier Malisse, who more than two hours earlier had looked on the point of collapse and been led off the court by the doctor, had responded so impressively on his return that he and David Nalbandian were locked at two sets all when, at 8.57 pm, they were sent home for the night because of fading light.

Malisse, the pony-tailed Belgian, who had knocked out Yevgeny Kafelnikov and Greg Rusedski along the way, was known to have suffered with a racing heart in the past and mid-way through the first half, after chasing to deliver several typically vigorous backhands from the baseline, he began clutching his chest and breathing deeply.

Although he initially continued after a brief delay while he consulted the doctor, at the end of the set which he lost in a 7-2 tie-break, he called for more health-care advice and this time left the court for what became a much extended medical time-out because of the time needed to diagnose the problem. The doctor's official report talked of Malisse feeling 'breathless, dizzy and generally unwell'. A call was also made to his doctor in Belgium who confirmed that the player had suffered similar symptoms in the past when under stress and it was safe for him to continue playing.

By the time rain brought Malisse additional respite of well over an hour, Nalbandian had moved to a 4-2 lead in the second

Xavier Malisse (above) was soon under pressure from David Nalbandian in the second semi-final.

Far left: Tim Henman's grim disappointment is plain as he still manages to offer a thank-you salute to the crowd.

Drama on No. 1 Court where Xavier Malisse began anxiously clutching his chest, and then had to be helped off court at the end of the first-set tie-break with a racing heartbeat during his match against an impressive David Nalbandian.

set but, when they resumed, the Argentine's serve began to lose some of its sting, his forehand lost much of its authority and the Belgian began his astonishing recovery.

Nalbandian had been upset by what he regarded as the unreasonable amount of time Malisse had been allowed. 'Is he going to stop ten minutes each time?' he pleaded with umpire Pascal Maria as the crowd's growing unrest was also apparent. Several times Nalbandian asked the umpire 'Won't he have to retire?' Although the regulations allow three minutes for treatment during a medical time-out, there is no stipulation as to how much time can be taken while the problem is diagnosed. By Wimbledon 2003 that will probably have been clarified.

John McEnroe always used to say that playing doubles was the finest form of practice for the singles and that idea clearly found favour with the Williams sisters as they wound up their preparations for another meeting against each other in the ladies' singles final the following day by sweeping majestically into a semi-final of the doubles.

Venus and Serena, who first won the doubles title two years earlier, took only 52 minutes to outclass the Slovenian pair, Tina Krizan and Katarina Srebotnik 6-2, 6-0. 'We like to think that once we've broken serve we've won the set' said Venus, chillingly.

Otherwise, because of the weather, there was limited progress on the outside courts. In the men's doubles, Mark Knowles and Daniel Nestor reached the final by beating the Bryan brothers, Bob and Mike, in an amazing match of three tie-breaks and only three games in which there were break points — one either way in the first set, and one in which the Bryans had two chances in the third. In the other semi-final, the holders, Don Johnson and Jared Palmer were unfinished at one set all against Todd Woodbridge and Jonas Bjorkman.

THE CHAMPIONSHIPS WIMBLEDON

SATURDAY 6 JULY

day 12

day 12 • ladies' final

Serena Williams (left) takes off for another mighty forehand winner in the ladies' singles final; while Mrs Oracene (Brandi) Williams, mother of both finalists, watched proudly from the players' box (below); the sisters pose before the start (bottom) with Shayna Godin of the National Asthma Campaign.

Serena Williams could hardly contain her excitement at the end of a power-packed ladies' singles final in which she inherited the title from her sister, Venus, and recorded another piece of Wimbledon history.

'At the beginning of the year I said "you know, I don't care what happens this year, I want to win Wimbledon" ' she revealed. 'It was an extra bonus for me to win the French. All I'd really been thinking about was winning Wimbledon. I wanted to become a member of so much prestige and to be part of history.'

It had taken the younger sister just 78 minutes to beat Venus 7-6, 6-3 in the most competitive of the nine matches there had been between them. Her success made it the first time that the names of two sisters will forever be engraved on the trophy, while at the same time destroyed Venus's bid to become only the ninth player in the history of The Championships to win the ladies' singles title three times in succession.

As usual for their matches, the atmosphere was more muted than when other players are involved because most spectators are reluctant to take sides in what they regard as an intimate family affair. At least, though, on this occasion, despite the one-dimensional style of play, with one ferocious strike after another, the power, accuracy and persistence of the tennis had to be admired.

In both her two previous finals, Venus had astonished everyone by hitting serves around the 120 mph mark. This time the pace was often very much slower and it seemed clear that she was being restricted by a strain in the shoulder considerably more than she was willing to admit.

As Serena said later 'I knew beforehand it was hurting but she never has an excuse for anything. She can be so stubborn. You have to respect her not only as a sister but also a person for not everyone would do that. Unfortunately, when you're in a match, it's a war out there and if there's a weakness, someone's going to have to be attacked.'

The first set was fiercely competitive but with a fair number of unforced errors also thrown in at unexpected moments, which largely explained why there were four breaks of serve on the way to the tie-break.

day 12 · ladies' final

In this, although Venus won the first point, she netted twice to trail 3-6 and Serena took the 44-minute first set at the second opportunity with a serve which stood as an ace after neither player heard the 'let' call which umpire Jane Harvey actually made twice, after the line monitor had bleeped.

Serena admitted that the first she knew anything about a 'let' was when Martina Navratilova told her afterwards in the locker room. 'I don't think it was a let. I think the machine made a mistake' she said, and then, when asked if Venus knew about the incident, replied with a chuckle 'I don't know, I'm not going to tell her.'

Serena had a chance to race away with the second set when she held in the opening game and had two chances to break in the second. Similarly she failed to build on her break from 4-2 at a time when Venus's serve was beginning to falter. From 30-30 in the seventh game, a mishit cross-court forehand by Venus was transformed into a spectacularly angled winner and then, moments after a cry from the stand had requested 'three sets, Serena,' that briefly became a possibility when the younger sister netted a tame backhand and was pegged back to 4-3.

Although Serena seemed to be breathing heavily at this stage, as if the pressure of the occasion as well as the tireless running and

retrieving by the defending champion was taking its toll, it was actually Venus who was in trouble.

Serving at 15-30, in the eighth game, she shaped up to make a rare approach to the net and netted a rushed forehand. Even worse, two points later, a second serve at 67 mph dropped into the wrong court. Serena did not need to be asked twice to serve out for the title and was soon dancing and waving for joy as Venus left her to take centre stage.

The match, which was surely competitive enough to end, once and for all, the innuendos — fiercely denied by both girls and their father — that sometimes his opinion as to who should win on a particular day has been more influential than it should be, took 74 minutes and gave Serena her third Grand Slam success. 'I think it's time I also won the Australian' she added with an almost permanent twinkle in the eyes. It was her moment, her day and she was determined to enjoy every minute.

When serving for the match, Serena had taken some time to compose herself and she played it perfectly, pausing again briefly at 30-0 before completing the task with two more of her most formidable serves. 'I wanted to win so badly' she said. 'I told myself "It's now or never." It's hard to beat Venus, you know.'

Above left: Serena and Venus embrace after the match.

Venus (above) fought hard but, after two years as champion, had to watch Serena receive the trophy from HRH Princess Alexandra, accompanied by Christopher Gorringe (centre), Chief Executive of the All England Club, and her brother, HRH The Duke of Kent, President of the All England Club.

Serena Williams talking about the inspirational messages she had written to herself that she was reading under her towel at changeovers:
'Just reminders of things I need to work on... just simple things because normally I lose focus when I sit down and start to look around. Venus doesn't have that problem.'

Left: Venus and Serena discuss where they want to play the next shot in the ladies' doubles final in which Serena's stretch volleys helped them to beat Anna Kournikova and Chanda Rubin (right).

The success of the Williams sisters did not end there. The 20- and 22-year-old daughters of a former Louisiana cotton-picker, who insists that it was because he saw how much money there was to be won on the WTA Tour that, from the age of four, he deliberately trained them to be tennis champions, were back on court barely an hour later in the semi-finals of the ladies' doubles.

Wimbledon's Centre Court is a world away from the public courts in a poor district of Los Angeles where their careers began but they have adjusted confidently to their elite status. Although they lost the first set against Anna Kournikova and Chanda Rubin as Venus tried to settle back in after the disappointment of losing the singles crown, they swept through to the final, 6-7, 6-0, 6-3.

Kournikova, who could have been forgiven for casting envious glances at the two players who have taken over at the top of the rankings while her game, though clearly talented, had been withering on the vine, was the best of the four in the first set. The drop shot, with which she secured points for the set, was a delight. Once Rubin had dropped her serve at the start of the second set, however, the Williams girls took over.

At a time when the doubles circuits on both the men's and women's tours were having to fight, if not for their existence, then certainly for the respect and the recognition they felt they deserved, the second Saturday of The Championships provided a perfect opportunity for doubles tennis to shine in the front window.

Not that it brought much joy to Kournikova. She also lost in the quarter finals of the mixed doubles when she and Jonas Bjorkman were beaten 6-4, 6-2 by India's supreme doubles player, Mahesh Bhupathi and the Russian, Elena Likhovtseva. It was also Bjorkman's second appearance of the day but he at least had the consolation of knowing that he and Todd Woodbridge, who is almost omni-present on such occasions, were already through to the men's doubles final after winning a thrilling semi-final from two sets down against defending champions, Don Johnson and Jared Palmer, 7-5, 4-6, 6-7, 7-5, 6-2.

day 13 • men's final

Previous spread: Lleyton Hewitt poses as if to say 'It's mine and I intend to keep it' while David Nalbandian is in reflective mood as he admires the runner-up's salver.

Top left: The finalists pose with Richard Bowden, proudly representing the Barnardo's charity, who was chosen to toss a special £5 coin, presented by the Royal Mint to celebrate the Queen's Golden Jubilee, to decide which player served first.

Right: The action was watched over by British umpire, Mike Morrisey, while Australian fans made 'The Hill' their territory for the afternoon.

15 years after Lleyton Hewitt, back home in Adelaide, watched on television as Pat Cash became the last Australian to win Wimbledon and then clambered up into the player's box to family and friends, he repeated the achievement and the celebration.

Both tasks were completed more straight-forwardly than in 1987. Cash had to contend with Ivan Lendl, the reigning US Open and French Open champion. David Nalbandian was an Argentine rookie who had become the first player to reach the Wimbledon final at his first attempt since the American, Dick Savitt, in 1951.

That was not the only difference. Cash had to clamber over bodies in the old stand-ing enclosure and then precariously scale the roof of a television commentary box to reach his destination. Now there are steps offering a far less hazardous route.

Hewitt, who had initially hesitated by his chair after going through the customary for-malities of commiserating with his opponent and shaking hands with umpire, Mike Mor-risey, after his victory, said 'I had no idea what I was going to do if I won. I went back to my chair and then thought "Stuff it! I'll go and do it." It's been 15 years since an Aussie won, so I thought I'd copy him out there.'

Despite often looking more nervous than at any time in the fortnight and having cer-tainly made more errors than against Tim Henman in the semi-finals, Hewitt always did enough to show why he was the best player in the world and deny the personable as well as talented Nalbandian, making more than a noble challenge.

The 6-1, 6-3, 6-2 scoreline, after 1 hour 57 minutes, was scant reward for Nalbandian, the least likely finalist since Wilhelm Bungert in the last all-amateur Wimbledon in 1967. For the 20-year-old, who had emerged from a section of the draw where Pete Sampras had been expected to set the pace, it was a daunt-ing experience. Not only was it his first Grand Slam final but his first tournament on grass and, because of the way the schedule had been disturbed by the weather, it was also the first time he had been listed to compete on the Centre Court. All that on top of knowing that the top-seeded world number one, who had

beaten him on his favourite clay surface in their only previous meeting three months earlier, was on the other side of the net.

He did his best in this youngest Wimbledon men's singles final in the Open era and that, surely, is as much as anyone could ask. The crowd certainly understood and roared their support and approval whenever he gave them the opportunity to do so, especially during a period in the second set when things looked as if they might just be in the balance. One hopes that his progress will encourage other South Americans and Spaniards to realise in future years that a few weeks spent competing on grass each year need not be time wasted; indeed, as Nalbandian demonstrated, the opposite.

To give Nalbandian at least some feel of what playing on the Centre Court might be like, he was allowed to practice on it for 45 minutes in the morning of the final but even with that the odds were stacked heavily against him and the contest, which was twice interrupted by rain and delayed briefly by a male streaker, was more of an occasion than a match.

When Nalbandian double faulted on the first point on his way to being broken in the opening game and Hewitt raced away without much resistance to a 4-0 lead, there were fears that it might become even more one-sided than when a youthful Jimmy Connors, 22, overwhelmed Ken Rosewall, a few months short of Rosewall's 40th birthday, in 1974. Rosewall, like Chris Lewis against John McEnroe in 1983 and now Nalbandian, won six games.

Hard though he tried, Nalbandian was never in a position to inject more than fleeting atmosphere into the match. Yet between the two rain breaks, beginning immediately after Hewitt had held for 1-0 in the second set, there was a half-hour spell, as the score advanced to 3-3, 30-30 on the Hewitt serve, when he gave as good as he got.

The point with which he wiped out the service break Hewitt had earned in the second game of the set was one of the best of the day. Twice the Australian failed to put away overheads and then Nalbandian played an exquisite lob winner after stretching well to cover his opponent's angled drop shot.

For a time, Hewitt seemed strangely subdued, partly because, although the overwhelming favourite, his first Wimbledon final was also a major test for him. His first-serve percentage dropped, his forehands, that earlier had been ripping glorious cross-court winners, faltered. He also found himself increasingly being drawn into rallies of 20 strokes or more, the majority of which Nalbandian was winning, often by biding his time while he forced Hewitt into the backhand corner and then whipped over a stinging forehand.

Once they returned after the second disruption of 33 minutes, though, Hewitt quickly struck decisively. Having held to lead 4-3, he stepped up the pace to attack with such relish in the next game that he broke Nalbandian and then served out for the set. The beginning of the end for the Argentine came when, having broken back to 2-2 in the third set with another of his many superb backhands down the line, he immediately lost his own serve in the next game when he was clearly upset by two baseline decisions, both shown to be correct on the television replays, at opposite ends of the court.

Hewitt was the youngest champion since Boris Becker and it gave him special pleasure when he looked up towards the opposite end of the court and saw the German in the commentary box watching the title going to the player who had beaten him, also on the Centre Court, in his last singles match at The Championships. 'Winning Wimbledon is something I've dreamt about for as long as I can remember' said Hewitt, who called it 'proof to every kid playing in the local club in Australia that dreams can come true if you work hard enough to make them happen.'

That night, at The Champions' Dinner, when Frank Sedgman, Neale Fraser and Ken Rosewall were among the legendary Australians in attendance, paying tribute to their fellow countryman, Hewitt — described by the All England Club Chairman Tim Phillips as 'the fastest player in the game with top spin lobs the rest of us dream about' — said: 'Wimbledon means so much to Australians and Australia has such a great tradition here that it means so much to me.'

Serena Williams and Lleyton
Hewitt were honoured at the
Champions' Dinner

ingles

The Williams sisters could jointly celebrate the ladies' doubles title while (left) Australian Todd Reid won the boys' singles title from Algerian, Lamine Ouahab (above).

Below left: Vera Douchevina on the way to beating Maria Sharapova (below) in the all-Russian junior girls' final.

Such an endorsement from the present as well as former generations of top players was underlined by the presence of almost all the winners and runners-up of every event, including the juniors. The only exceptions were those in the final of the mixed doubles, who had still been on court at 8.35 pm when the first of the diners were well on their way to The Savoy.

The mixed doubles title went, after a fluctuating final, 6-2, 1-6, 6-1, to Elena Likhovtseva from Russia and India's Mahesh Bhupathi, over Daniela Hantuchova, one of the previous year's winners from Slovakia and her new partner, Kevin Ullyett from Zimbabwe.

Earlier the doubles finals, as with the men's singles, followed an expected path. Todd Woodbridge, who had won the title for a record six times with Mark Woodforde, added a seventh when he and Sweden's Jonas Bjorkman won an entertaining 2 hours 35 minutes match against defending champions, Don Johnson and Jared Palmer from the United States.

Watched by Woodforde, who was commentating for viewers back home in Australia, the new combination quickly asserted their superiority and impressively brushed off the

setback of losing the third-set tie-break to win 6-1, 6-2, 6-7, 7-5.

The Williams sisters completed what Venus called 'a great six weeks for us' (also spanning Roland Garros) by beating Paola Suarez of the Argentine and Virginia Ruano-Pascual, her Spanish partner, 6-2, 7-5.

Although Venus and Serena both lost their serves and trailed 2-4 in the second set, they then sharpened both the pace and power of their game and took control. Serena admitted to 'suffering a little tightness' after beating Venus in the singles final the day before. She said she was 'grateful that Venus exercised a calming influence on me to make sure there was no upset here. I didn't want to let her down.'

Taking his cue from Hewitt, fifth-seeded Todd Reid took the junior boys' singles title back to Australia when he beat Lamine Ouahab from Algeria 7-6, 6-4, while the boys' doubles was won by the Romanians, Florin Mergea and Horia Tecau, who beat the Americans, Rajeev Ram and Brian Baker, 6-4, 4-6, 6-4.

In an all-Russian final to the girls' singles, Vera Douchevina recovered from a tense start to beat Maria Sharapova, 4-6, 6-1, 6-2, while in the doubles, Kim Clijsters' younger sister, Elke, confirmed her growing potential by taking the title with Barbora Strycova from the Czech Republic, 6-4, 5-7, 8-6, against the American-German partnership of Ally Baker and Anna-Lena Groenefeld.

Britain at least had success in the men's 45-and-over Invitation Doubles when Buster Mottram and Colin Dowdeswell beat the Americans, Peter Fleming and Sandy Mayer, 7-5, 6-4 in the final. The 35-and-over Invitation Doubles went to the Americans, Scott Davis and David Pate, who beat Britain's Jeremy Bates and Nick Fulwood, while the ladies' 35-and-over Invitation Doubles final saw Mima Jausovec from Slovenia and the American, Gretchen Magers, beat Ros Nideffer of South Africa and Helena Sukova of the Czech Republic, 6-3, 6-3.

With that the curtain came down on Wimbledon 2002, the 116th staging of The Championships and one which had attracted the second largest attendance in its history. Roll on Wimbledon 2003, June 23–July 6.

The Ladies' Singles Championship

Serena Williams

The Gentlemen's Doubles Championship

Jonas Bjorkman & Todd Woodbridge

The Mixed Doubles Championship

Mahesh Bhupathi & Elena Likhovtseva

The Ladies' Doubles Championship

Serena Williams & Venus Williams

The Gentlemen's Singles Championship

Lleyton Hewitt

The 35 and over Ladies' Invitation Doubles

Gretchen Magers & Mima Jausovec

The Girls' Doubles Championship

Elke Clijsters & Barbora Strycova

The Boys' Doubles Championship

Florin Mergea & Horia Tecau

The Girls' Singles Championship

Vera Douchevina

The Boys' Singles Championship

Todd Reid

The 45 and over Gentlemen's Invitation Doubles

Colin Dowdeswell & Buster Mottram

The 35 and over Gentlemen's Invitation Doubles

Scott Davis & David Pate

CHAMPIONSHIP
RECORDS
2002

ALPHABETICAL LIST OF COMPETITORS

LADIES

82 Ahl Miss L.A. *(Great Britain)*
Arendt Miss N. *(USA)*
75 Arn Miss G. *(Germany)*
Asagoe Miss S. *(Japan)*
Augustus Miss A. *(USA)*
28 Baltacha Miss E. *(Great Britain)*
Barclay Miss C. *(Australia)*
66 Barna Miss A. *(Germany)*
89 Bedanova Miss D. *(Czech Republic)*
11 Beigbeder Miss C. *(France)*
79 Benesova Miss I. *(Czech Republic)*
34 Bes Miss E. *(Spain)*
58 Black Miss C. *(Zimbabwe)*
Boogert Miss K. *(Netherlands)*
118 Bovina Miss E. *(Russia)*
92 Brandi Miss K. *(USA)*
123 Callens Miss E.S.H. *(Belgium)*
96 Capriati Miss J. *(USA)*
59 Casanova Miss M. *(Switzerland)*
122 Cervanova Miss L. *(Slovak Republic)*
62 Chladkova Miss D. *(Czech Republic)*
32 Clijsters Miss K. *(Belgium)*
25 Coetzer Miss A.J. *(South Africa)*
21 Collin Miss H. *(Great Britain)*
7 Craybas Miss J. *(USA)*
Crook Miss H. *(Great Britain)*
86 Daniilidou Miss E. *(Greece)*
Davies Miss V.E. *(Great Britain)*
De Villiers Miss N. *(South Africa)*
104 Dechy Miss N. *(France)*
49 Dementieva Miss E. *(Russia)*
Dhenin Miss C. *(France)*
103 Diaz-Oliva Miss M. *(Argentina)*
97 Dokic Miss J. *(Yugoslavia)*
127 Dominikovic Miss E. *(Australia)*
5 Drake Miss M. *(Canada)*
Dulko Miss G. *(Argentina)*
74 Dyrberg Miss E. *(Denmark)*
Embry Miss J. *(USA)*
17 Farina Elia Mrs S. *(Italy)*
121 Fernandez Miss C. *(Argentina)*
Fokina Miss G. *(Russia)*
100 Foretz Miss S. *(France)*
18 Frazier Miss A. *(USA)*
Freye Miss K. *(Germany)*
Fujiwara Miss R. *(Japan)*
84 Fusai Miss A. *(France)*
22 Gagliardi Miss E. *(Switzerland)*
43 Garbin Miss T. *(Italy)*
35 Gersi Miss A. *(Czech Republic)*
78 Grande Miss R. *(Italy)*
Grandin Miss N. *(South Africa)*
Grant Miss K. *(South Africa)*
71 Granville Miss L. *(USA)*
26 Gubacsi Miss Z. *(Hungary)*
112 Hantuchova Miss D. *(Slovak Republic)*
Hawkins Miss A. *(Great Britain)*
64 Henin Miss J. *(Belgium)*
Hiraki Miss R. *(Japan)*
19 Hopkins Miss J. *(USA)*
99 Hrdlickova Miss K. *(Czech Republic)*
Huber Mrs L. *(South Africa)*
95 Husarova Miss J. *(Slovak Republic)*
45 Irvin Miss M. *(USA)*
93 Jidkova Miss A. *(Russia)*
44 Kandarr Miss J. *(Germany)*
38 Keothavong Miss A. *(Great Britain)*
Kolbovic Miss R. *(Canada)*
85 Kostanic Miss J. *(Croatia)*
119 Kournikova Miss A. *(Russia)*
105 Kremer Miss A. *(Luxembourg)*
Krizan Miss T. *(Slovenia)*
Kuznetsova Miss S. *(Russia)*
50 Lamade Miss B. *(Germany)*
51 Lee Miss J. *(Chinese Taipei)*
106 Leon Garcia Miss G. *(Spain)*
30 Likhovtseva Miss E. *(Russia)*
52 Loit Miss E. *(France)*
56 Majoli Miss I. *(Croatia)*
24 Maleeva Miss M. *(Bulgaria)*
125 Mandula Miss P. *(Hungary)*
94 Marrero Miss M. *(Spain)*
Martincova Miss E. *(Czech Republic)*
12 Martinez Miss C. *(Spain)*
107 Matevzic Miss M. *(Slovenia)*
80 Mauresmo Miss A. *(France)*
McNeil Miss L.M. *(USA)*
McQuillan Miss R. *(Australia)*
McShea Miss L. *(Australia)*
6 Mikaelian Miss M-G. *(Switzerland)*
Miyagi Miss N. *(Japan)*
67 Molik Miss A. *(Australia)*
Montalvo Miss L. *(Argentina)*
102 Montolio Miss A. *(Spain)*
61 Muller Miss M. *(Germany)*
Musgrave Miss T. *(Australia)*
73 Myskina Miss A. *(Russia)*
60 Nagyova Miss H. *(Slovak Republic)*
Navratilova Miss M. *(USA)*
36 Neffa-De Los Rios Mrs R. *(Paraguay)*
14 Nejedly Miss J. *(Canada)*
Nemeckova Miss L. *(Czech Republic)*
90 Noorlander Miss S. *(Netherlands)*
2 O'Donoghue Miss J. *(Great Britain)*
87 Obata Miss S. *(Japan)*
39 Ondraskova Miss Z. *(Czech Republic)*
83 Oremans Miss M. *(Netherlands)*
110 Osterloh Miss L. *(USA)*
Ostrovskaya Miss N. *(Belarus)*
120 Panova Miss T. *(Russia)*
10 Perebiynis Miss T. *(Ukraine)*
68 Pierce Miss M. *(France)*
55 Pisnik Miss T. *(Slovenia)*
Po-Messerli Mrs K. *(USA)*
101 Poutchek Miss T. *(Belarus)*
13 Prakusya Miss W. *(Indonesia)*
72 Pratt Miss N.J. *(Australia)*
108 Pullin Miss J.M. *(Great Britain)*
16 Raymond Miss L.M. *(USA)*
37 Razzano Miss V. *(France)*
31 Reeves Miss S. *(USA)*
63 Rippner Miss B. *(USA)*
20 Rittner Miss B. *(Germany)*
Rodionova Miss A. *(Russia)*
3 Roesch Miss A. *(Germany)*
4 Ruano Pascual Miss V. *(Spain)*
116 Rubin Miss C. *(USA)*
42 Sanchez Lorenzo Miss M. *(Spain)*
57 Schett Miss B. *(Austria)*
126 Schiavone Miss F. *(Italy)*
Schlukebir Miss K. *(USA)*
9 Schnyder Miss P. *(Switzerland)*
124 Schwartz Miss B. *(Austria)*
33 Seles Miss M. *(USA)*
76 Selyutina Miss I. *(Kazakhstan)*
Sequera Miss M. *(Venezuela)*
77 Serna Miss M. *(Spain)*
117 Serra Zanetti Miss A. *(Italy)*
54 Serra Zanetti Miss A. *(Italy)*
91 Sfar Miss S. *(Tunisia)*
81 Shaughnessy Miss M. *(USA)*
48 Smashnova Miss A. *(Israel)*
Spears Miss A. *(USA)*
15 Srebotnik Miss K. *(Slovenia)*
Steck Miss J. *(South Africa)*
88 Stevenson Miss A. *(USA)*
Stewart Miss B. *(Australia)*
Stubbs Miss R.P. *(Australia)*
8 Suarez Miss P. *(Argentina)*
109 Sucha Miss M. *(Slovak Republic)*
40 Sugiyama Miss A. *(Japan)*
115 Svensson Mrs A. *(Sweden)*
114 Talaja Miss S. *(Croatia)*
41 Tanasugarn Miss T. *(Thailand)*
Tarabini Miss P. *(Argentina)*
98 Tatarkova Miss E. *(Ukraine)*
Tauziat Miss N. *(France)*
65 Testud Miss S. *(France)*
111 Torrens Valero Miss C. *(Spain)*
46 Tu Miss M. *(USA)*
113 Tulyaganova Miss I. *(Uzbekhistan)*
Van Exel Miss A. *(Netherlands)*
Vanc Miss A. *(Romania)*
27 Vento-Kabchi Mrs M. *(Venezuela)*
29 Vinci Miss R. *(Italy)*
23 Viollet Miss R. *(Great Britain)*
Vis Miss C.M. *(Netherlands)*
Wartusch Miss P. *(Austria)*
70 Weingartner Miss M. *(Germany)*
Wheeler Miss C. *(Australia)*
47 Widjaja Miss A. *(Indonesia)*
128 Williams Miss S. *(USA)*
1 Williams Miss V. *(USA)*
Woodroffe Miss L.A. *(Great Britain)*
Zaric Miss D. *(Yugoslavia)*
69 Zvereva Miss N. *(Belarus)*
53 Zvonareva Miss V. *(Russia)*

GENTLEMEN

13 Acasuso J. *(Argentina)*
Adams D. *(South Africa)*
96 Agassi A. *(USA)*
31 Ancic M. *(Croatia)*
55 Arazi H. *(Morocco)*
Arnold L. *(Argentina)*
110 Arthurs W. *(Australia)*
Aspelin S. *(Sweden)*
34 Bachelot J-F. *(France)*
85 Balcells J. *(Spain)*
Barnard M. *(South Africa)*
99 Bastl G. *(Switzerland)*
116 Beck K. *(Slovak Republic)*
Bertolini M. *(Italy)*
Bhupathi M. *(India)*
2 Bjorkman J. *(Sweden)*
Black B. *(Zimbabwe)*
Black W. *(Zimbabwe)*
89 Blake J. *(USA)*
71 Blanco G. *(Spain)*
15 Bogdanovic A. *(Great Britain)*
84 Boutter J. *(France)*
Bowen D. *(USA)*
58 Bower J. *(South Africa)*
Braasch K. *(Germany)*
Brandi C. *(Italy)*
94 Brasington J. *(USA)*
Bryan B. *(USA)*
Bryan M. *(USA)*
22 Burgsmuller L. *(Germany)*
26 Calleri A. *(Argentina)*
49 Canas G. *(Argentina)*
35 Caratti C. *(Italy)*
114 Carlsen K. *(Denmark)*
3 Carraz G. *(France)*
Cermak F. *(Czech Republic)*
21 Chang M. *(USA)*
88 Chela J.I. *(Argentina)*
Childs L. *(Great Britain)*
Cibulec T. *(Czech Republic)*
102 Clavet F. *(Spain)*
123 Clement A. *(France)*
Coetzee J. *(South Africa)*
27 Coutelot N. *(France)*
117 Cowan B. *(Great Britain)*
Crichton T. *(Australia)*
Damm M. *(Czech Republic)*
45 Davydenko N. *(Russia)*
De Jager J-L. *(South Africa)*
119 Delgado J. *(Great Britain)*
39 Delgado R. *(Paraguay)*
106 Dent T. *(USA)*
36 Draper S. *(Australia)*
59 Dupuis A. *(France)*
Eagle J. *(Australia)*
52 Economidis K. *(Greece)*
48 El Aynaoui Y. *(Morocco)*
Ellwood B. *(Australia)*
81 Enqvist T. *(Sweden)*
Erlich J. *(Israel)*
16 Escude N. *(France)*
Etlis G. *(Argentina)*
32 Federer R. *(Switzerland)*
Ferreira E. *(South Africa)*
38 Ferreira W. *(South Africa)*
17 Ferrero J.C. *(Spain)*
Fish M. *(USA)*
Fisher A. *(Australia)*
Florent A. *(Australia)*
Friedl L. *(Czech Republic)*
Fukarek O. *(Czech Republic)*
78 Galvani S. *(Italy)*
108 Gambill J-M. *(USA)*
Garcia M. *(Argentina)*
62 Gaudenzi A. *(Italy)*
9 Gaudio G. *(Argentina)*
Gimelstob J. *(USA)*
18 Godwin N. *(South Africa)*
Goellner M-K. *(Germany)*
29 Golmard J. *(France)*
100 Golovanov D. *(Russia)*
87 Gonzalez F. *(Chile)*
10 Guzman J-P. *(Argentina)*
Haarhuis P. *(Netherlands)*
Hadad A. *(Israel)*
Haggard C. *(South Africa)*
Hanley P. *(Australia)*
Healey N. *(Australia)*
33 Henman T. *(Great Britain)*
1 Hewitt L. *(Australia)*
Hill M. *(Australia)*
Hilton M.A. *(Great Britain)*
68 Hipfl M. *(Austria)*
Hood M. *(Argentina)*
66 Hrbaty D. *(Slovak Republic)*
Humphries S. *(USA)*
Huss S. *(Australia)*
64 Johansson T. *(Sweden)*
Johnson D. *(USA)*
65 Kafelnikov Y. *(Russia)*
Kendrick R. *(USA)*
Kerr J. *(Australia)*
86 Kiefer N. *(Germany)*
Kitinov A. *(Macedonia)*
5 Knowle J. *(Austria)*
Knowles M. *(Bahamas)*
Koenig R. *(South Africa)*
50 Kohlmann M. *(Germany)*
57 Koubek S. *(Austria)*
91 Krajicek R. *(Netherlands)*
46 Kratochvil M. *(Switzerland)*
Kratzmann A. *(Australia)*
47 Labadze I. *(Georgia)*
Landsberg J. *(Sweden)*
120 Lapentti N. *(Ecuador)*
70 Larsson M. *(Sweden)*
Leach R. *(USA)*
75 Lee H-T. *(Korea Republic)*
98 Lee M. *(Great Britain)*
Levinsky J. *(Czech Republic)*
95 Levy H. *(Israel)*
40 Ljubicic I. *(Croatia)*
6 Llodra M. *(France)*
Lobo L. *(Argentina)*
51 Lopez F. *(Spain)*
Luxa P. *(Czech Republic)*
7 Mackin A.R. *(Great Britain)*
Macpherson D. *(Australia)*
MacPhie B. *(USA)*
72 Malisse X. *(Belgium)*
4 Mamiit C. *(USA)*
Marray J. *(Great Britain)*
77 Martin A. *(Spain)*
121 Martin T. *(USA)*
107 Massu N. *(Chile)*
101 Mathieu P-H. *(France)*
111 Meligeni F. *(Brazil)*
Melo D. *(Brazil)*
74 Melzer J. *(Austria)*
Merklein M. *(Bahamas)*
Milligan L. *(Great Britain)*
105 Mirnyi M. *(Belarus)*
124 Montanes A. *(Spain)*
20 Morrison J. *(USA)*
104 Nalbandian D. *(Argentina)*
Nestor D. *(Canada)*
8 Nieminen J. *(Finland)*
112 Novak J. *(Czech Republic)*
19 Okun N. *(Israel)*
Olhovskiy A. *(Russia)*
Oliver G. *(USA)*
Orsanic D. *(Argentina)*
Paes L. *(India)*
Pala P. *(Czech Republic)*
Palmer J. *(USA)*
82 Parmar A. *(Great Britain)*
113 Pavel A. *(Romania)*
Perry T. *(Australia)*
Petrovic D. *(Australia)*
83 Philippoussis M. *(Australia)*
127 Pioline C. *(France)*
23 Pless K. *(Denmark)*
37 Portas A. *(Spain)*
Prinosil D. *(Germany)*
Qureshi A-U-H. *(Pakistan)*
Rikl D. *(Czech Republic)*
41 Robredo T. *(Spain)*
125 Rochus C. *(Belgium)*
126 Rochus O. *(Belgium)*
80 Roddick A. *(USA)*
Rodriguez M. *(Argentina)*
Roitman S. *(Argentina)*
Rosner P. *(South Africa)*
14 Rosset M. *(Switzerland)*
73 Rusedski G. *(Great Britain)*
109 Russell M. *(USA)*
60 Sa A. *(Brazil)*
128 Safin M. *(Russia)*
97 Sampras P. *(USA)*
103 Sanchez D. *(Spain)*
122 Sanguinetti D. *(Italy)*
25 Santoro F. *(France)*
63 Saretta F. *(Brazil)*
54 Sargsian S. *(Armenia)*
44 Saulnier C. *(France)*
118 Savolt A. *(Hungary)*
24 Schalken S. *(Netherlands)*
Schneiter A. *(Argentina)*
56 Schuettler R. *(Germany)*
Sherwood D. *(Great Britain)*
Shimada T. *(Japan)*
Silcock G. *(Australia)*
115 Simoni A. *(Brazil)*
Skoch D. *(Czech Republic)*
42 Sluiter R. *(Netherlands)*
69 Spadea V. *(USA)*
Spencer K. *(Great Britain)*
92 Squillari F. *(Argentina)*
93 Srichaphan P. *(Thailand)*
43 Stepanek R. *(Czech Republic)*
76 Stoliarov A. *(Russia)*
Stolle S. *(Australia)*
Suk C. *(Czech Republic)*
Tarango J. *(USA)*
67 Thomann N. *(France)*
Thomas J. *(USA)*
Trifu G. *(Romania)*
79 Ulihrach B. *(Czech Republic)*
Ullyett K. *(Zimbabwe)*
Vacek D. *(Czech Republic)*
30 Vacek J. *(Czech Republic)*
11 Vahaly B. *(USA)*
Vanhoudt T. *(Belgium)*
53 Vicente F. *(Spain)*
Vizner P. *(Czech Republic)*
28 Voinea A. *(Romania)*
Voltchkov V. *(Belarus)*
Wakefield M. *(South Africa)*
61 Waske A. *(Germany)*
Wassen R. *(Netherlands)*
Weiner G. *(USA)*
Woodbridge T.A. *(Australia)*
12 Youzhny M. *(Russia)*
90 Zabaleta M. *(Argentina)*
Zimonjic N. *(Yugoslavia)*
Zovko L. *(Croatia)*

GIRLS

3 Anderson Miss K. *(South Africa)*
41 Avants Miss C. *(USA)*
18 Babos Miss Z. *(Hungary)*
24 Baker Miss A. *(USA)*
63 Barnes Miss A. *(Great Britain)*
9 Bastrikova Miss A. *(Russia)*
40 Bauer Miss S. *(Netherlands)*
48 Birnerova Miss E. *(Czech Republic)*
46 Blocker Miss K. *(Germany)*
4 Casanova Miss D. *(Switzerland)*
49 Cetkovska Miss P. *(Czech Republic)*
5 Clijsters Miss E. *(Belgium)*
26 Correa Miss M. *(Ecuador)*
27 Czafikova Miss K. *(Slovak Republic)*
Dellacqua Miss C. *(Australia)*
55 Devidze Miss S. *(Georgia)*
59 Domachowska Miss M. *(Poland)*
32 Douchevina Miss V. *(Russia)*
Falcon Miss M. *(USA)*
52 Flavell Miss F. *(Great Britain)*
34 Gajdosova Miss J. *(Slovak Republic)*
8 Golovin Miss T. *(France)*
28 Grady Miss H. *(Great Britain)*
16 Groenefeld Miss A-L. *(Germany)*
50 Gullickson Miss C. *(USA)*
6 Hawkins Miss A. *(Great Britain)*
15 Hlavackova Miss A. *(Czech Republic)*
64 Hsieh Miss S-W. *(Chinese Taipei)*
13 Ismailova Miss I. *(Uzbekhistan)*
37 Ivanov Miss D. *(Australia)*
57 Ivanovic Miss A. *(Yugoslavia)*
38 Jackson Miss J. *(USA)*
35 Khalifa Miss A. *(Egypt)*
56 Kirilenko Miss M. *(Russia)*
25 Klepac Miss A. *(Slovenia)*
19 Kuryanovich Miss I. *(Belarus)*
47 Laine Miss E. *(Finland)*
44 Laosirichon Miss P. *(Thailand)*
20 Linetskaya Miss E. *(Russia)*
2 Liu Miss A. *(USA)*
23 Lyubtsova Miss O. *(Ukraine)*
7 Mirza Miss S. *(India)*
12 Miseviciute Miss A. *(Lithuania)*
14 Mueller Miss A. *(Great Britain)*
36 O'Brien Miss K. *(Great Britain)*
58 Oprandi Miss R. *(Switzerland)*
54 Ozegovic Miss N. *(Croatia)*
21 Rankin Miss R. *(Great Britain)*
31 Rao Miss S. *(USA)*
61 Robinson Miss S. *(USA)*
30 Sema Miss Y. *(Japan)*
33 Sharapova Miss M. *(Russia)*
60 Smolenakova Miss L. *(Slovak Republic)*
62 Sourkova Miss A. *(Russia)*
10 South Miss M. *(Great Britain)*
Stanciute Miss L. *(Lithuania)*
57 Stosur Miss S. *(Australia)*
17 Strycova Miss B. *(Czech Republic)*
29 Tamaela Miss E. *(Netherlands)*
11 Tanaka Miss S. *(Japan)*
1 Tavares Miss M. *(Brazil)*
45 Teller Miss P. *(Hungary)*
39 Terblanche Miss T. *(South Africa)*
Van Boekel Miss D. *(Netherlands)*
42 Vialiamovskaia Miss M. *(Russia)*
43 Webley-Smith Miss E. *(Great Britain)*
22 Welford Miss T. *(Australia)*
51 Zawacki Miss T. *(USA)*

BOYS

Amritraj S. *(USA)*
17 Baghdatis M. *(Cyprus)*
9 Baker B. *(USA)*
14 Balazs G. *(Hungary)*
20 Bayer M. *(Germany)*
57 Berdych T. *(Czech Republic)*
40 Bogdanovic A. *(Great Britain)*
6 Bonatto A. *(Brazil)*
11 Brewer D. *(Great Britain)*
36 Brown D. *(Jamaica)*
Burn T. *(Great Britain)*
52 Cohen J. *(USA)*
18 Crawley N. *(Great Britain)*
64 Dabul B. *(Argentina)*
15 Dancevic F. *(Canada)*
25 Darcis S. *(Belgium)*
10 Durek R. *(Australia)*
45 Evans B. *(USA)*
47 Evans C. *(Great Britain)*
Feeney A. *(Australia)*
32 Felder M. *(Uruguay)*
34 Ferreiro F. *(Brazil)*
22 Gabashvili T. *(Russia)*
30 Goodall J. *(Great Britain)*
42 Gregorc L. *(Slovenia)*
51 Guccione C. *(Australia)*
35 Haybittel R. *(Australia)*
46 Henry R. *(Australia)*
Hung B. *(Hong Kong)*
62 Hutchins R. *(Great Britain)*
Jelovac B. *(Great Britain)*
4 Juska A. *(Latvia)*
13 Kanev Y. *(Bulgaria)*
19 Kapun A. *(Slovenia)*
2 Koning M. *(Netherlands)*
7 Kuseta D. *(Croatia)*
61 Kwon C. *(USA)*
59 Liu T-W. *(Chinese Taipei)*
29 Loglo K. *(Togo)*
Lowe M. *(Great Britain)*
26 Lustig D. *(Czech Republic)*
55 Mergea F. *(Romania)*
Miotto A. *(Great Britain)*
24 Montcourt M. *(France)*
48 Morel C. *(France)*
37 Murray A. *(Great Britain)*
63 Nadal-Parera R. *(Spain)*
33 Ouahab L. *(Algeria)*
49 Petzschner P. *(Germany)*
31 Przysiezny M. *(Poland)*
5 Ram R. *(USA)*
16 Reid T. *(Australia)*
Rufer B. *(Switzerland)*
43 Ruiz A. *(Mexico)*
60 Ryderstedt M. *(Sweden)*
Saengsuwarn S. *(Thailand)*
44 Searle R. *(Great Britain)*
41 Sela D. *(Israel)*
Shimizu S. *(Japan)*
39 Sitak A. *(Russia)*
38 Skrypko A. *(Belarus)*
21 Smeets R. *(Australia)*
3 Smith M. *(Great Britain)*
58 Soeda G. *(Japan)*
28 Sottocorno A. *(Bolivia)*
23 Stiegwardt M. *(Ecuador)*
53 Tecau H. *(Romania)*
54 Thomas G. *(Great Britain)*
8 Tsonga J. *(France)*
50 Van Der Valk B. *(Netherlands)*
56 Vilarrubi M. *(Uruguay)*
1 Wang Y-T. *(Chinese Taipei)*
12 Westerhof C. *(South Africa)*
27 Yim R. *(USA)*
Yu H-T. *(Hong Kong)*

Bold figures denote position in Singles Draw

The winner becomes the holder, for the year only, of the CHALLENGE CUP presented by The All England Lawn Tennis and Croquet Club. The winner receives a silver replica of the Challenge Cup. A silver salver is presented to the runner-up and a bronze medal to each defeated semi-finalist.

Heavy type denotes seeded players. The figure in brackets against names denotes the order in which they have been seeded. (W) = Wild card. (Q) = Qualifier. (L) = Lucky loser.

The matches are the best of five sets

THE GENTLEMEN'S DOUBLES CHAMPIONSHIP

Holders: D. Johnson and J. Palmer

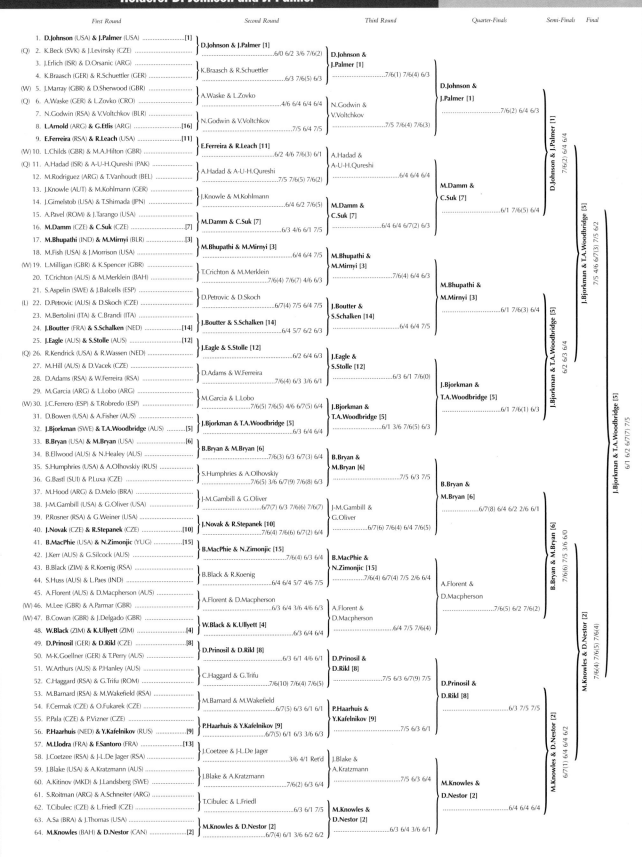

	First Round	Second Round	Third Round	Quarter-Finals	Semi-Finals	Final

1. **D.Johnson** (USA) & **J.Palmer** (USA) ....[1]
(Q) 2. K.Beck (SVK) & J.Levinsky (CZE) ....
   D.Johnson & J.Palmer [1] ......6/0 6/2 3/6 7/6(2)
3. J.Erlich (ISR) & D.Orsanic (ARG) ....
4. K.Braasch (GER) & R.Schuettler (GER) ....
   K.Braasch & R.Schuettler ......6/3 7/6(5) 6/3
   D.Johnson & J.Palmer [1] ......7/6(1) 7/6(4) 6/3
(W) 5. J.Marray (GBR) & D.Sherwood (GBR) ....
(Q) 6. A.Waske (GER) & L.Zovko (CRO) ....
   A.Waske & L.Zovko 4/6 6/4 6/4 6/4
7. N.Godwin (RSA) & V.Voltchkov (BLR) ....
8. **L.Arnold** (ARG) & **G.Etlis** (ARG) ....[16]
   N.Godwin & V.Voltchkov 7/5 6/4 7/5
   N.Godwin & V.Voltchkov ......7/5 7/6(4) 7/6(3)
   D.Johnson & J.Palmer [1] ......7/6(2) 6/4 6/3

9. **E.Ferreira** (RSA) & **R.Leach** (USA) ....[11]
(W) 10. L.Childs (GBR) & M.A.Hilton (GBR) ....
   E.Ferreira & R.Leach [11] ......6/2 4/6 7/6(3) 6/1
(Q) 11. A.Hadad (ISR) & A-U-H.Qureshi (PAK) ....
12. M.Rodriguez (ARG) & T.Vanhoudt (BEL) ....
   A.Hadad & A-U-H.Qureshi ......7/5 7/6(5) 7/6(2)
   A.Hadad & A-U-H.Qureshi 6/4 6/4 6/4
13. J.Knowle (AUT) & M.Kohlmann (GER) ....
14. J.Gimelstob (USA) & T.Shimada (JPN) ....
   J.Knowle & M.Kohlmann ......6/4 6/2 7/6(5)
   M.Damm & C.Suk [7] ......6/4 6/4 6/7(2) 6/3
15. A.Pavel (ROM) & J.Tarango (USA) ....
16. **M.Damm** (CZE) & **C.Suk** (CZE) ....[7]
   M.Damm & C.Suk [7] 6/3 4/6 6/1 7/5
   M.Damm & C.Suk [7] ......6/1 7/6(5) 6/4

17. **M.Bhupathi** (IND) & **M.Mirnyi** (BLR) ....[3]
18. M.Fish (USA) & J.Morrison (USA) ....
   M.Bhupathi & M.Mirnyi [3] 6/4 6/4 7/5
(W) 19. L.Milligan (GBR) & K.Spencer (GBR) ....
20. T.Crichton (AUS) & M.Merklein (BAH) ....
   T.Crichton & M.Merklein ......7/6(4) 7/6(7) 4/6 6/3
   M.Bhupathi & M.Mirnyi [3] ......7/6(4) 6/4 6/3
21. S.Aspelin (SWE) & J.Balcells (ESP) ....
(L) 22. D.Petrovic (AUS) & D.Skoch (CZE) ....
   D.Petrovic & D.Skoch ......6/7(4) 7/5 6/4 7/5
23. M.Bertolini (ITA) & C.Brandi (ITA) ....
24. **J.Boutter** (FRA) & **S.Schalken** (NED) ....[14]
   J.Boutter & S.Schalken [14] 6/4 5/7 6/2 6/3
   J.Boutter & S.Schalken [14] 6/4 6/4 7/5
   M.Bhupathi & M.Mirnyi [3] ......6/1 7/6(3) 6/4

25. **J.Eagle** (AUS) & **S.Stolle** (AUS) ....[12]
(Q) 26. R.Kendrick (USA) & R.Wassen (NED) ....
   J.Eagle & S.Stolle [12] 6/2 6/4 6/4
27. M.Hill (AUS) & D.Vacek (CZE) ....
28. D.Adams (RSA) & W.Ferreira (RSA) ....
   D.Adams & W.Ferreira ......7/6(4) 6/3 3/6 6/1
   J.Eagle & S.Stolle [12] ......6/3 6/1 7/6(0)
29. M.Garcia (ARG) & L.Lobo (ARG) ....
(W) 30. J.C.Ferrero (ESP) & T.Robredo (ESP) ....
   M.Garcia & L.Lobo ......7/6(5) 7/6(5) 4/6 6/7(5) 6/4
   J.Bjorkman & T.A.Woodbridge [5] ......6/1 7/6(1) 6/3
31. D.Bowen (USA) & A.Fisher (AUS) ....
32. **J.Bjorkman** (SWE) & **T.A.Woodbridge** (AUS) ....[5]
   J.Bjorkman & T.A.Woodbridge [5] 6/3 6/4 6/4
   J.Bjorkman & T.A.Woodbridge [5] ......6/1 3/6 7/6(5) 6/3
   J.Bjorkman & T.A.Woodbridge [5] 6/2 6/3 6/4

33. **B.Bryan** (USA) & **M.Bryan** (USA) ....[6]
34. B.Ellwood (AUS) & N.Healey (AUS) ....
   B.Bryan & M.Bryan [6] ......7/6(3) 6/3 6/7(3) 6/4
35. S.Humphries (USA) & A.Olhovskiy (RUS) ....
36. G.Bastl (SUI) & P.Luxa (CZE) ....
   S.Humphries & A.Olhovskiy ......7/6(5) 3/6 6/7(9) 7/6(8) 6/3
   B.Bryan & M.Bryan [6] 7/5 6/3 7/5
37. M.Hood (ARG) & D.Melo (BRA) ....
38. J-M.Gambill (USA) & G.Oliver (USA) ....
   J-M.Gambill & G.Oliver ......6/7(3) 6/3 7/6(6) 7/6(7)
   J-M.Gambill & G.Oliver ......6/7(6) 7/6(4) 6/4 7/6(5)
39. P.Rosner (RSA) & G.Weiner (USA) ....
40. **J.Novak** (CZE) & **R.Stepanek** (CZE) ....[10]
   J.Novak & R.Stepanek [10] ......7/6(4) 7/6(6) 6/7(2) 6/4
   B.Bryan & M.Bryan [6] ......6/7(8) 6/4 6/2 2/6 6/1

41. **B.MacPhie** (USA) & **N.Zimonjic** (YUG) ....[15]
42. J.Kerr (AUS) & G.Silcock (AUS) ....
   B.MacPhie & N.Zimonjic [15] ......7/6(4) 6/3 6/4
43. B.Black (ZIM) & R.Koenig (RSA) ....
44. S.Huss (AUS) & L.Paes (IND) ....
   B.Black & R.Koenig 6/4 6/4 5/7 4/6 7/5
   B.MacPhie & N.Zimonjic [15] ......7/6(4) 6/7(4) 7/5 2/6 6/4
45. A.Florent (AUS) & D.Macpherson (AUS) ....
(W) 46. M.Lee (GBR) & A.Parmar (GBR) ....
   A.Florent & D.Macpherson 6/3 6/4 3/6 4/6 6/3
   A.Florent & D.Macpherson ......6/4 7/5 7/6(4)
(W) 47. B.Cowan (GBR) & J.Delgado (GBR) ....
48. **W.Black** (ZIM) & **K.Ullyett** (ZIM) ....[4]
   W.Black & K.Ullyett [4] 6/3 6/4 6/4
   A.Florent & D.Macpherson ......7/6(5) 6/2 7/6(2)

49. **D.Prinosil** (GER) & **D.Rikl** (CZE) ....[8]
50. M-K.Goellner (GER) & T.Perry (AUS) ....
   D.Prinosil & D.Rikl [8] 6/3 6/1 4/6 6/1
51. W.Arthurs (AUS) & P.Hanley (AUS) ....
52. C.Haggard (RSA) & G.Trifu (ROM) ....
   C.Haggard & G.Trifu ......7/6(10) 7/6(4) 7/6(5)
   D.Prinosil & D.Rikl [8] ......7/5 6/3 6/7(9) 7/5
53. M.Barnard (RSA) & M.Wakefield (RSA) ....
54. F.Cermak (CZE) & O.Fukarek (CZE) ....
   M.Barnard & M.Wakefield ......6/7(5) 6/3 6/1 6/1
   P.Haarhuis & Y.Kafelnikov [9] 7/5 6/3 6/1
55. P.Pala (CZE) & P.Vizner (CZE) ....
56. **P.Haarhuis** (NED) & **Y.Kafelnikov** (RUS) ....[9]
   P.Haarhuis & Y.Kafelnikov [9] ......6/7(5) 6/1 6/3 3/6 6/3
   D.Prinosil & D.Rikl [8] 6/3 7/5 7/5

57. **M.Llodra** (FRA) & **F.Santoro** (FRA) ....[13]
58. J.Coetzee (RSA) & J-L.De Jager (RSA) ....
   J.Coetzee & J-L.De Jager ......3/6 4/1 Ret'd
59. J.Blake (USA) & A.Kratzmann (AUS) ....
60. A.Kitinov (MKD) & J.Landsberg (SWE) ....
   J.Blake & A.Kratzmann ......7/6(2) 6/3 6/4
   J.Blake & A.Kratzmann 7/5 6/3 6/4
61. S.Roitman (ARG) & A.Schneiter (ARG) ....
62. T.Cibulec (CZE) & L.Friedl (CZE) ....
   T.Cibulec & L.Friedl 6/3 6/1 7/5
   M.Knowles & D.Nestor [2] 6/4 4/4 6/4
63. A.Sa (BRA) & J.Thomas (USA) ....
64. **M.Knowles** (BAH) & **D.Nestor** (CAN) ....[2]
   M.Knowles & D.Nestor [2] ......6/7(4) 6/1 3/6 6/2 6/2
   M.Knowles & D.Nestor [2] 6/3 6/4 3/6 6/1

D.Johnson & J.Palmer [1] ......7/5 4/6 6/7(3) 7/5 6/2

J.Bjorkman & T.A.Woodbridge [5] ......7/5 4/6 6/7(3) 7/5 6/2

M.Knowles & D.Nestor [2] ......7/6(1) 6/4 6/4 6/2

B.Bryan & M.Bryan [6] ......7/6(6) 7/5 3/6 6/0

M.Knowles & D.Nestor [2] ......7/6(4) 7/6(5) 7/6(4)

J.Bjorkman & T.A.Woodbridge [5] ......6/1 6/2 6/7(7) 7/5

Heavy type denotes seeded players. The figure in brackets against names denotes the order in which they have been seeded. (W) = Wild card. (Q) = Qualifier. (L) = Lucky loser.

The matches are the best of five sets

The winner becomes the holder, for the year only, of the CHALLENGE TROPHY presented by The All England Lawn Tennis and Croquet Club. The winner receives a silver replica of the Trophy. A silver salver is presented to the runner-up and a bronze medal to each defeated semi-finalist.

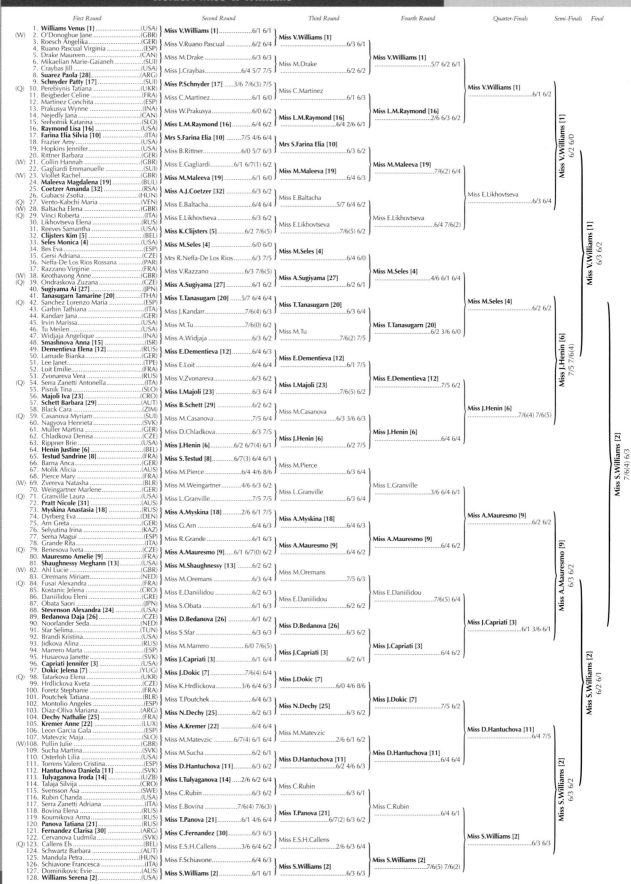

	First Round
	1. **Williams Venus [1]** (USA)
(W)	2. O'Donoghue Jane (GBR)
	3. Roesch Angelika (GER)
	4. Ruano Pascual Virginia (ESP)
	5. Drake Maureen (CAN)
	6. Mikaelian Marie-Gaianeh (SUI)
	7. Craybas Jill (USA)
	8. **Suarez Paola [28]** (ARG)
	9. **Schnyder Patty [17]** (SUI)
(Q)	10. Perebiynis Tatiana (UKR)
	11. Beigbeder Celine (FRA)
	12. Martinez Conchita (ESP)
	13. Prakusya Wynne (INA)
	14. Nejedly Jana (CAN)
	15. Srebotnik Katarina (SLO)
	16. **Raymond Lisa [16]** (USA)
	17. **Farina Elia Silvia [10]** (ITA)
	18. Frazier Amy (USA)
	19. Hopkins Jennifer (USA)
	20. Rittner Barbara (GER)
(W)	21. Collin Hannah (GBR)
	22. Gagliardi Emmanuelle (SUI)
(W)	23. Viollet Rachel (GBR)
	24. **Maleeva Magdalena [19]** (BUL)
	25. **Coetzer Amanda [32]** (RSA)
	26. Gubacsi Zsofia (HUN)
(Q)	27. Vento-Kabchi Maria (VEN)
(W)	28. Baltacha Elena (GBR)
(Q)	29. Vinci Roberta (ITA)
	30. Likhovtseva Elena (RUS)
	31. Reeves Samantha (USA)
	32. **Clijsters Kim [5]** (BEL)
	33. **Seles Monica [4]** (USA)
	34. Bes Eva (ESP)
	35. Gersi Adriana (CZE)
	36. Neffa-De Los Rios Rossana (PAR)
	37. Razzano Virginie (FRA)
(W)	38. Keothavong Anne (GBR)
(Q)	39. Ondraskova Zuzana (CZE)
	40. **Sugiyama Ai [27]** (JPN)
	41. **Tanasugarn Tamarine [20]** (THA)
(Q)	42. Sanchez Lorenzo Maria (ESP)
	43. Garbin Tathiana (ITA)
	44. Kandarr Jana (GER)
	45. Irvin Marissa (USA)
	46. Tu Meilen (USA)
	47. Widjaja Angelique (INA)
	48. **Smashnova Anna [15]** (ISR)
	49. **Dementieva Elena [12]** (RUS)
	50. Lamade Bianka (GER)
	51. Lee Janet (TPE)
	52. Loit Emilie (FRA)
	53. Zvonareva Vera (RUS)
	54. Serra Zanetti Antonella (ITA)
(Q)	55. Pisnik Tina (SLO)
	56. **Majoli Iva [23]** (CRO)
	57. **Schett Barbara [29]** (AUT)
	58. Black Cara (ZIM)
(Q)	59. Casanova Myriam (SUI)
	60. Nagyova Henrieta (SVK)
	61. Muller Martina (GER)
	62. Chladkova Denisa (CZE)
	63. Rippner Brie (USA)
	64. **Henin Justine [6]** (BEL)
	65. **Testud Sandrine [8]** (FRA)
	66. Barna Anca (GER)
	67. Molik Alicia (AUS)
	68. Pierce Mary (FRA)
(W)	69. Zvereva Natasha (BLR)
	70. Weingartner Marlene (GER)
(Q)	71. Granville Laura (USA)
	72. **Pratt Nicole [31]** (AUS)
	73. **Myskina Anastasia [18]** (RUS)
	74. Dyrberg Eva (DEN)
	75. Arn Greta (GER)
	76. Selyutina Irina (KAZ)
	77. Serna Magui (ESP)
	78. Grande Rita (ITA)
(Q)	79. Benesova Iveta (CZE)
	80. **Mauresmo Amelie [9]** (FRA)
	81. **Shaughnessy Meghann [13]** (USA)
(W)	82. Ahl Lucie (GBR)
	83. Oremans Miriam (NED)
(Q)	84. Fusai Alexandra (FRA)
	85. Kostanic Jelena (CRO)
	86. Daniilidou Eleni (GRE)
	87. Obata Saori (JPN)
	88. **Stevenson Alexandra [24]** (USA)
	89. **Bedanova Daja [26]** (CZE)
	90. Noorlander Seda (NED)
	91. Sfar Selima (TUN)
	92. Brandi Kristina (USA)
	93. Jidkova Alina (RUS)
	94. Marrero Marta (ESP)
	95. Husarova Janette (SVK)
	96. **Capriati Jennifer [3]** (USA)
	97. **Dokic Jelena [7]** (YUG)
(Q)	98. Tatarkova Elena (UKR)
	99. Hrdlickova Kveta (CZE)
	100. Foretz Stephanie (FRA)
	101. Poutchek Tatiana (BLR)
	102. Montolio Angeles (ESP)
	103. Diaz-Oliva Mariana (ARG)
	104. **Dechy Nathalie [25]** (FRA)
	105. **Kremer Anne [22]** (LUX)
	106. Leon Garcia Gala (ESP)
	107. Matevzic Maja (SLO)
(W)	108. Pullin Julie (GBR)
	109. Sucha Martina (SVK)
	110. Osterloh Lilia (USA)
	111. Torrens Valero Cristina (ESP)
	112. **Hantuchova Daniela [11]** (SVK)
	113. **Tulyaganova Iroda [14]** (UZB)
	114. Talaja Silvija (CRO)
	115. Svensson Asa (SWE)
	116. Rubin Chanda (USA)
	117. Serra Zanetti Adriana (ITA)
	118. Bovina Elena (RUS)
	119. Kournikova Anna (RUS)
	120. **Panova Tatiana [21]** (RUS)
	121. **Fernandez Clarisa [30]** (ARG)
	122. Cervanova Ludmila (SVK)
(Q)	123. Callens Els (BEL)
	124. Schwartz Barbara (AUT)
	125. Mandula Petra (HUN)
	126. Schiavone Francesca (ITA)
	127. Dominikovic Evie (AUS)
	128. **Williams Serena [2]** (USA)

Second Round

Miss V.Williams [1] 6/1 6/1 — Miss V.Ruano Pascual 6/2 6/4 — Miss M.Drake 6/1 6/0 — Miss J.Craybas 6/4 5/7 7/5 — Miss P.Schnyder [17] 3/6 7/6(3) 7/5 — Miss C.Martinez 6/1 6/0 — Miss W.Prakusya 6/0 6/2 — Miss L.M.Raymond [16] 6/4 6/2 — Mrs S.Farina Elia [10] 7/5 4/6 6/4 — Miss B.Rittner 6/0 5/7 6/3 — Miss E.Gagliardi 6/1 6/7(1) 6/2 — Miss M.Maleeva [19] 6/1 6/0 — Miss A.J.Coetzer [32] 6/3 6/2 — Miss E.Baltacha 6/4 6/4 — Miss E.Likhovtseva 6/3 6/2 — Miss K.Clijsters [5] 6/2 7/6(5) — Miss M.Seles [4] 6/0 6/0 — Mrs R.Neffa-De Los Rios 6/3 7/5 — Miss V.Razzano 6/3 7/6(5) — Miss A.Sugiyama [27] 6/1 6/2 — Miss T.Tanasugarn [20] 5/7 6/4 6/4 — Miss J.Kandarr 7/6(4) 6/3 — Miss M.Tu 7/6(0) 6/2 — Miss A.Widjaja 6/3 6/2 — Miss E.Dementieva [12] 6/4 6/3 — Miss E.Loit 6/4 6/4 — Miss V.Zvonareva 6/3 6/2 — Miss I.Majoli [23] 6/3 6/4 — Miss B.Schett [29] 6/2 6/2 — Miss M.Casanova 7/5 6/4 — Miss D.Chladkova 6/3 7/5 — Miss J.Henin [6] 6/2 6/7(4) 6/1 — Miss S.Testud [8] 6/7(3) 6/4 6/1 — Miss M.Pierce 6/4 4/6 8/6 — Miss M.Weingartner 4/6 6/3 6/2 — Miss L.Granville 7/5 7/5 — Miss A.Myskina [18] 2/6 6/1 7/5 — Miss G.Arn 6/4 6/3 — Miss R.Grande 6/1 6/3 — Miss A.Mauresmo [9] 6/1 6/7(0) 6/2 — Miss M.Shaughnessy [13] 6/2 6/2 — Miss M.Oremans 6/3 6/4 — Miss E.Daniilidou 6/2 6/3 — Miss S.Obata 6/1 6/3 — Miss D.Bedanova [26] 6/1 6/2 — Miss S.Sfar 6/3 6/3 — Miss M.Marrero 6/0 7/6(5) — Miss J.Capriati [3] 6/2 6/1 — Miss J.Dokic [7] 7/6(4) 6/4 — Miss K.Hrdlickova 3/6 6/4 6/4 — Miss T.Poutchek 6/4 6/3 — Miss N.Dechy [25] 6/2 6/3 — Miss A.Kremer [22] 6/4 6/4 — Miss M.Matevzic 6/7(4) 6/1 6/4 — Miss M.Sucha 6/2 6/1 — Miss D.Hantuchova [11] 6/3 6/2 — Miss I.Tulyaganova [14] 2/6 6/2 6/4 — Miss C.Rubin 6/3 6/2 — Miss E.Bovina 7/6(4) 7/6(3) — Miss T.Panova [21] 6/1 4/6 6/4 — Miss C.Fernandez [30] 6/3 6/3 — Miss E.S.H.Callens 3/6 6/4 6/2 — Miss F.Schiavone 6/4 6/3 — Miss S.Williams [2] 6/1 6/1

Third Round

Miss V.Williams [1] 6/3 6/1 — Miss C.Martinez 6/1 6/3 — Mrs S.Farina Elia [10] 6/3 6/2 — Miss M.Maleeva [19] 6/4 6/3 — Miss E.Baltacha 5/7 6/4 6/2 — Miss E.Likhovtseva 7/6(5) 6/2 — Miss M.Seles [4] 6/4 6/0 — Miss A.Sugiyama [27] 6/2 6/1 — Miss T.Tanasugarn [20] 6/3 6/4 — Miss M.Tu 7/6(2) 7/5 — Miss E.Dementieva [12] 6/1 7/5 — Miss I.Majoli [23] 7/6(5) 6/2 — Miss M.Casanova 6/3 3/6 6/3 — Miss J.Henin [6] 6/2 7/5 — Miss M.Pierce 6/3 6/4 — Miss L.Granville 6/3 6/4 — Miss A.Myskina [18] 6/4 6/3 — Miss A.Mauresmo [9] 6/4 6/2 — Miss M.Oremans 7/5 6/4 — Miss E.Daniilidou 6/2 6/2 — Miss D.Bedanova [26] 6/3 6/2 — Miss J.Capriati [3] 6/2 6/1 — Miss J.Dokic [7] 6/0 4/6 8/6 — Miss N.Dechy [25] 6/3 6/2 — Miss M.Matevzic 2/6 6/1 6/2 — Miss D.Hantuchova [11] 6/2 4/6 6/3 — Miss C.Rubin 6/3 6/1 — Miss T.Panova [21] 7/6(2) 6/3 6/2 — Miss E.S.H.Callens 2/6 6/3 6/4 — Miss S.Williams [2] 6/3 6/3

Fourth Round

Miss V.Williams [1] 5/7 6/2 6/1 — Miss L.M.Raymond [16] 2/6 6/3 6/2 — Miss M.Maleeva [19] 7/6(2) 6/4 — Miss E.Likhovtseva 6/4 7/6(2) — Miss M.Seles [4] 4/6 6/1 6/4 — Miss T.Tanasugarn [20] 6/2 3/6 6/0 — Miss E.Dementieva [12] 7/5 6/2 — Miss J.Henin [6] 6/4 6/4 — Miss L.Granville 3/6 6/4 6/1 — Miss A.Mauresmo [9] 6/4 6/2 — Miss E.Daniilidou 7/6(5) 6/4 — Miss J.Capriati [3] 6/4 6/2 — Miss J.Dokic [7] 7/5 6/2 — Miss D.Hantuchova [11] 6/4 6/4 — Miss C.Rubin 6/4 6/1 — Miss S.Williams [2] 7/6(5) 7/6(2)

Quarter-Finals

Miss V.Williams [1] 6/1 6/2 — Miss E.Likhovtseva 6/3 6/4 — Miss M.Seles [4] 6/2 6/2 — Miss J.Henin [6] 7/6(4) 7/6(5) — Miss A.Mauresmo [9] 6/2 6/2 — Miss J.Capriati [3] 6/1 3/6 6/1 — Miss D.Hantuchova [11] 6/4 7/5 — Miss S.Williams [2] 6/3 6/3

Semi-Finals

Miss V.Williams [1] 6/3 6/2 — Miss J.Henin [6] 7/5 7/6(4) — Miss A.Mauresmo [9] 6/3 6/2 — Miss S.Williams [2] 6/2 6/1

Final

Miss V.Williams [1] 6/2 6/0 — Miss S.Williams [2] 7/6(4) 6/3

Winner: Miss S.Williams [2] 6/3 6/2

Heavy type denotes seeded players. The figure in brackets against names denotes the order in which they are seeded. (W) = Wild card. (Q) = Qualifier. (L) = Lucky loser.

The matches are the best of three sets

THE LADIES' DOUBLES CHAMPIONSHIP

Holders: Miss L. M. Raymond and Miss R. P. Stubbs

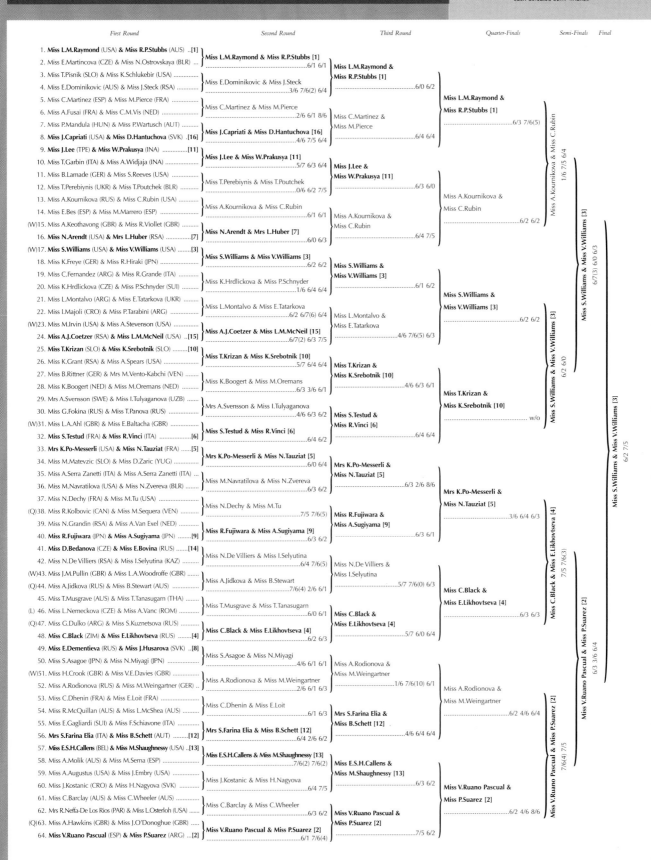

First Round	Second Round	Third Round	Quarter-Finals	Semi-Finals	Final

1. **Miss L.M.Raymond** (USA) & **Miss R.P.Stubbs** (AUS) ..[1]
2. Miss E.Martincova (CZE) & Miss N.Ostrovskaya (BLR) ...
   - **Miss L.M.Raymond & Miss R.P.Stubbs [1]** — 6/1 6/1
3. Miss T.Pisnik (SLO) & Miss K.Schlukebir (USA) ....
4. Miss E.Dominikovic (AUS) & Miss J.Steck (RSA) ....
   - Miss E.Dominikovic & Miss J.Steck — 3/6 7/6(2) 6/4
   - **Miss L.M.Raymond & Miss R.P.Stubbs [1]** — 6/0 6/2
5. Miss C.Martinez (ESP) & Miss M.Pierce (FRA) ....
6. Miss A.Fusai (FRA) & Miss C.M.Vis (NED) ....
   - Miss C.Martinez & Miss M.Pierce — 2/6 6/1 8/6
7. P.Mandula (HUN) & Miss P.Wartusch (AUT) ....
8. **Miss J.Capriati** (USA) & **Miss D.Hantuchova** (SVK) ..[16]
   - **Miss J.Capriati & Miss D.Hantuchova [16]** — 4/6 7/5 6/4
   - Miss C.Martinez & Miss M.Pierce — 6/4 6/4
   - **Miss L.M.Raymond & Miss R.P.Stubbs [1]** — 6/3 7/6(5)
9. **Miss J.Lee** (TPE) & **Miss W.Prakusya** (INA) ....[11]
10. Miss T.Garbin (ITA) & Miss A.Widjaja (INA) ....
    - **Miss J.Lee & Miss W.Prakusya [11]** — 5/7 6/3 6/4
11. Miss B.Lamade (GER) & Miss S.Reeves (USA) ....
12. Miss T.Perebiynis (UKR) & Miss T.Poutchek (BLR) ....
    - Miss T.Perebiynis & Miss T.Poutchek — 0/6 6/2 7/5
    - **Miss J.Lee & Miss W.Prakusya [11]** — 6/3 6/0
13. Miss A.Kournikova (RUS) & Miss C.Rubin (USA) ....
14. Miss E.Bes (ESP) & Miss M.Marrero (ESP) ....
    - Miss A.Kournikova & Miss C.Rubin — 6/1 6/1
    - Miss A.Kournikova & Miss C.Rubin — 6/2 6/2
15. (W) Miss A.Keothavong (GBR) & Miss R.Viollet (GBR) ....
16. **Miss N.Arendt** (USA) & **Mrs L.Huber** (RSA) ....[7]
    - **Miss N.Arendt & Mrs L.Huber [7]** — 6/0 6/3
    - Miss A.Kournikova & Miss C.Rubin — 6/4 7/5
    - Miss A.Kournikova & Miss C.Rubin — 1/6 7/5 6/4
17. (W) **Miss S.Williams** (USA) & **Miss V.Williams** (USA) ....[3]
18. Miss K.Freye (GER) & Miss H.Hiraki (JPN) ....
    - **Miss S.Williams & Miss V.Williams [3]** — 6/2 6/2
19. Miss C.Fernandez (ARG) & Miss R.Grande (ITA) ....
20. Miss K.Hrdlickova (CZE) & Miss P.Schnyder (SUI) ....
    - Miss K.Hrdlickova & Miss P.Schnyder — 1/6 6/4 6/4
    - **Miss S.Williams & Miss V.Williams [3]** — 6/1 6/0
21. Miss L.Montalvo (ARG) & Miss E.Tatarkova (UKR) ....
22. Miss I.Majoli (CRO) & Miss P.Tarabini (ARG) ....
    - Miss L.Montalvo & Miss E.Tatarkova — 6/2 6/7(6) 6/4
    - Miss L.Montalvo & Miss E.Tatarkova — 4/6 7/6(5) 6/3
23. (W) Miss M.Irvin (USA) & Miss A.Stevenson (USA) ....
24. **Miss A.J.Coetzer** (RSA) & **Miss L.M.McNeil** (USA) ..[15]
    - **Miss A.J.Coetzer & Miss L.M.McNeil [15]** — 6/7(2) 6/3 7/5
    - **Miss S.Williams & Miss V.Williams [3]** — 6/2 6/2
    - **Miss S.Williams & Miss V.Williams [3]** — 6/2 6/0
25. **Miss T.Krizan** (SLO) & **Miss K.Srebotnik** (SLO) ....[10]
26. Miss K.Grant (RSA) & Miss A.Spears (USA) ....
    - **Miss T.Krizan & Miss K.Srebotnik [10]** — 5/7 6/4 6/4
27. Miss B.Rittner (GER) & Mrs M.Vento-Kabchi (VEN) ....
28. Miss K.Boogert (NED) & Miss M.Oremans (NED) ....
    - Miss K.Boogert & Miss M.Oremans — 6/3 3/6 6/1
    - **Miss T.Krizan & Miss K.Srebotnik [10]** — 4/6 6/3 6/1
29. Mrs A.Svensson (SWE) & Miss I.Tulyaganova (UZB) ....
30. Miss G.Fokina (RUS) & Miss T.Panova (RUS) ....
    - Mrs A.Svensson & Miss I.Tulyaganova — 4/6 6/3 6/2
    - **Miss S.Testud & Miss R.Vinci [6]** — ...
31. (W) Miss L.A.Ahl (GBR) & Miss E.Baltacha (GBR) ....
32. **Miss S.Testud** (FRA) & **Miss R.Vinci** (ITA) ....[6]
    - **Miss S.Testud & Miss R.Vinci [6]** — 6/4 6/2
    - **Miss S.Testud & Miss R.Vinci [6]** — 6/4 6/4
    - **Miss T.Krizan & Miss K.Srebotnik [10]** — w/o
33. **Mrs K.Po-Messerli** (USA) & **Miss N.Tauziat** (FRA) ......[5]
34. Miss M.Matevzic (SLO) & Miss D.Zaric (YUG) ....
    - **Mrs K.Po-Messerli & Miss N.Tauziat [5]** — 6/0 6/1
35. Miss A.Serra Zanetti (ITA) & Miss A.Serra Zanetti (ITA) ...
36. Miss M.Navratilova (USA) & Miss N.Zvereva (BLR) ....
    - Miss M.Navratilova & Miss N.Zvereva — 6/3 6/2
    - **Mrs K.Po-Messerli & Miss N.Tauziat [5]** — 6/3 2/6 8/6
37. Miss N.Dechy (FRA) & Miss M.Tu (USA) ....
38. (Q) Miss R.Kolbovic (CAN) & Miss M.Sequera (VEN) ....
    - Miss N.Dechy & Miss M.Tu — 7/5 7/6(5)
    - **Mrs K.Po-Messerli & Miss N.Tauziat [5]** — 3/6 6/4 6/3
39. Miss N.Grandin (RSA) & Miss A.Van Exel (NED) ....
40. **Miss R.Fujiwara** (JPN) & **Miss A.Sugiyama** (JPN) ....[9]
    - **Miss R.Fujiwara & Miss A.Sugiyama [9]** — 6/3 6/2
    - **Miss R.Fujiwara & Miss A.Sugiyama [9]** — 6/3 6/1
41. **Miss D.Bedanova** (CZE) & **Miss E.Bovina** (RUS) ....[14]
42. Miss N.De Villiers (RSA) & Miss I.Selyutina (KAZ) ....
    - Miss N.De Villiers & Miss I.Selyutina — 6/4 7/6(5)
43. (W) Miss J.M.Pullin (GBR) & Miss L.A.Woodroffe (GBR) ......
44. (Q) Miss A.Jidkova (RUS) & Miss B.Stewart (AUS) ....
    - Miss A.Jidkova & Miss B.Stewart — 7/6(4) 2/6 6/1
    - Miss N.De Villiers & Miss I.Selyutina — 5/7 7/6(0) 6/3
45. Miss T.Musgrave (AUS) & Miss T.Tanasugarn (THA) ....
46. (L) Miss L.Nemeckova (CZE) & Miss A.Vanc (ROM) ....
    - Miss T.Musgrave & Miss T.Tanasugarn — 6/0 6/1
    - **Miss C.Black & Miss E.Likhovtseva [4]** — 6/3 6/3
47. (Q) Miss G.Dulko (ARG) & Miss S.Kuznetsova (RUS) ....
48. **Miss C.Black** (ZIM) & **Miss E.Likhovtseva** (RUS) ....[4]
    - **Miss C.Black & Miss E.Likhovtseva [4]** — 6/2 6/3
    - **Miss C.Black & Miss E.Likhovtseva [4]** — 5/7 6/0 6/4
    - **Miss C.Black & Miss E.Likhovtseva [4]** — 7/5 7/6(3)
49. **Miss E.Dementieva** (RUS) & **Miss J.Husarova** (SVK) ..[8]
50. Miss S.Asagoe (JPN) & Miss N.Miyagi (JPN) ....
    - Miss S.Asagoe & Miss N.Miyagi — 4/6 6/1 6/1
51. (W) Miss H.Crook (GBR) & Miss V.E.Davies (GBR) ....
52. Miss A.Rodionova (RUS) & Miss M.Weingartner (GER) ..
    - Miss A.Rodionova & Miss M.Weingartner — 2/6 6/1 6/3
    - Miss A.Rodionova & Miss M.Weingartner — 1/6 7/6(10) 6/1
53. Miss C.Dhenin (FRA) & Miss E.Loit (FRA) ....
54. Miss R.McQuillan (AUS) & Miss L.McShea (AUS) ....
    - Miss C.Dhenin & Miss E.Loit — 6/1 6/4
    - Miss A.Rodionova & Miss M.Weingartner — 6/2 4/6 6/4
55. Miss E.Gagliardi (SUI) & Miss F.Schiavone (ITA) ....
56. **Mrs S.Farina Elia** (ITA) & **Miss B.Schett** (AUT) ....[12]
    - **Mrs S.Farina Elia & Miss B.Schett [12]** — 6/4 2/6 6/2
    - **Mrs S.Farina Elia & Miss B.Schett [12]** — 4/6 6/4 6/4
    - **Miss V.Ruano Pascual & Miss P.Suarez [2]** — 6/3 3/6 6/4
57. **Miss E.S.H.Callens** (BEL) & **Miss M.Shaughnessy** (USA) ..[13]
58. Miss A.Molik (AUS) & Miss M.Serna (ESP) ....
    - **Miss E.S.H.Callens & Miss M.Shaughnessy [13]** — 7/6(4) 7/6(2)
59. Miss A.Augustus (USA) & Miss J.Embry (USA) ....
60. Miss J.Kostanic (CRO) & Miss H.Nagyova (SVK) ....
    - Miss J.Kostanic & Miss H.Nagyova — 6/4 7/5
    - **Miss E.S.H.Callens & Miss M.Shaughnessy [13]** — 6/3 6/2
61. Miss C.Barclay (AUS) & Miss C.Wheeler (AUS) ....
62. Mrs R.Neffa-De Los Rios (PAR) & Miss L.Osterloh (USA) ......
    - Miss C.Barclay & Miss C.Wheeler — 6/3 6/4
    - **Miss V.Ruano Pascual & Miss P.Suarez [2]** — 6/2 4/6 8/6
63. (Q) Miss A.Hawkins (GBR) & Miss J.O'Donoghue (GBR) ......
64. **Miss V.Ruano Pascual** (ESP) & **Miss P.Suarez** (ARG) ...[2]
    - **Miss V.Ruano Pascual & Miss P.Suarez [2]** — 6/1 7/6(4)
    - **Miss V.Ruano Pascual & Miss P.Suarez [2]** — 7/5 6/2
    - **Miss V.Ruano Pascual & Miss P.Suarez [2]** — 7/6(4) 7/5

Miss S.Williams & Miss V.Williams [3] — 6/2 7/5

Holders: L. Friedl and Miss D. Hantuchova

The winners become the holders, for the year only, of the CHALLENGE CUPS presented by the family of the late Mr S.H. SMITH. The winners receive silver replicas of the Challenge Cup. A silver salver is presented to each of the runners-up and a bronze medal to each defeated semi-finalist.

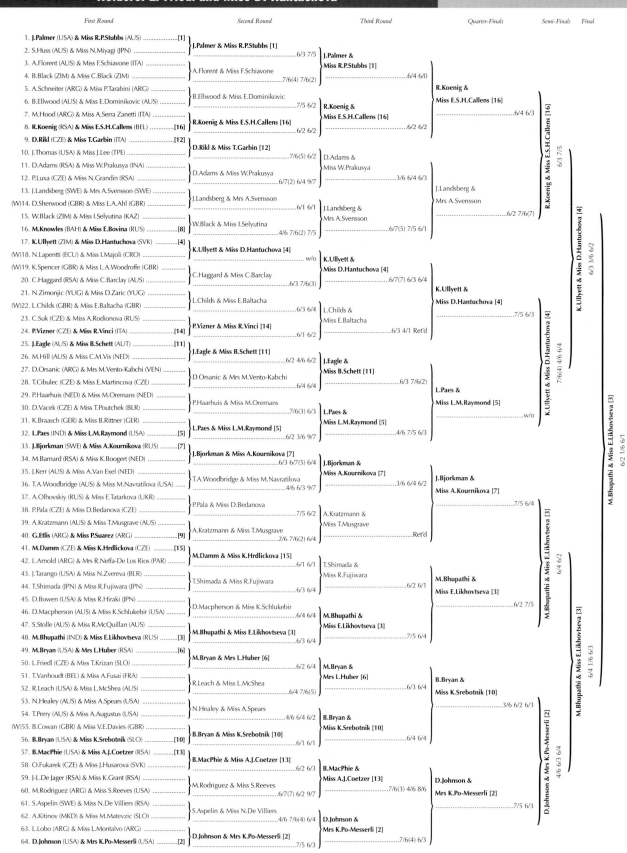

First Round	Second Round	Third Round	Quarter-Finals	Semi-Finals	Final

1. **J.Palmer** (USA) **& Miss R.P.Stubbs** (AUS) ....[1]
2. S.Huss (AUS) & Miss N.Miyagi (JPN) ....
 — J.Palmer & Miss R.P.Stubbs [1] 6/3 7/5
3. A.Florent (AUS) & Miss F.Schiavone (ITA) ....
4. B.Black (ZIM) & Miss C.Black (ZIM) ....
 — A.Florent & Miss F.Schiavone ....7/6(4) 7/6(2)
 — J.Palmer & Miss R.P.Stubbs [1] 6/4 6/0
5. A.Schneiter (ARG) & Miss P.Tarabini (ARG) ....
6. B.Ellwood (AUS) & Miss E.Dominikovic (AUS) ....
 — B.Ellwood & Miss E.Dominikovic 7/5 6/2
7. M.Hood (ARG) & Miss A.Serra Zanetti (ITA) ....
8. **R.Koenig** (RSA) **& Miss E.S.H.Callens** (BEL) ....[16]
 — R.Koenig & Miss E.S.H.Callens [16] 6/2 6/2
 — R.Koenig & Miss E.S.H.Callens [16] 6/2 6/2
 — R.Koenig & Miss E.S.H.Callens [16] 6/4 6/3
9. **D.Rikl** (CZE) **& Miss T.Garbin** (ITA) ....[12]
10. J.Thomas (USA) & Miss J.Lee (TPE) ....
 — D.Rikl & Miss T.Garbin [12] ....7/6(5) 6/2
11. D.Adams (RSA) & Miss W.Prakusya (INA) ....
12. P.Luxa (CZE) & Miss N.Grandin (RSA) ....
 — D.Adams & Miss W.Prakusya ....6/7(2) 6/4 9/7
 — D.Adams & Miss W.Prakusya 3/6 6/4 6/2
13. J.Landsberg (SWE) & Mrs A.Svensson (SWE) ....
(W)14. D.Sherwood (GBR) & Miss L.A.Ahl (GBR) ....
 — J.Landsberg & Mrs A.Svensson 6/1 6/1
15. W.Black (ZIM) & Miss I.Selyutina (KAZ) ....
16. **M.Knowles** (BAH) **& Miss E.Bovina** (RUS) ....[8]
 — W.Black & Miss I.Selyutina ....4/6 7/6(2) 7/5
 — J.Landsberg & Mrs A.Svensson ....6/7(5) 7/5 6/1
 — J.Landsberg & Mrs A.Svensson ....6/2 7/6(7)
 — R.Koenig & Miss E.S.H.Callens [16] 6/3 7/5
17. **K.Ullyett** (ZIM) **& Miss D.Hantuchova** (SVK) ....[4]
(W)18. N.Lapentti (ECU) & Miss I.Majoli (CRO) ....
 — K.Ullyett & Miss D.Hantuchova [4] ....w/o
19. K.Spencer (GBR) & Miss L.A.Woodroffe (GBR) ....(W)
20. C.Haggard (RSA) & Miss C.Barclay (AUS) ....
 — C.Haggard & Miss C.Barclay ....6/3 7/6(3)
 — K.Ullyett & Miss D.Hantuchova [4] ....6/7(7) 6/3 6/4
21. N.Zimonjic (YUG) & Miss D.Zaric (YUG) ....
(W)22. L.Childs (GBR) & Miss E.Baltacha (GBR) ....
 — L.Childs & Miss E.Baltacha 6/3 6/4
23. C.Suk (CZE) & Miss A.Rodionova (RUS) ....
24. **P.Vizner** (CZE) **& Miss R.Vinci** (ITA) ....[14]
 — P.Vizner & Miss R.Vinci [14] 6/1 6/2
 — L.Childs & Miss E.Baltacha ....6/3 4/1 Ret'd
 — K.Ullyett & Miss D.Hantuchova [4] 7/5 6/3
 — K.Ullyett & Miss D.Hantuchova [4] 6/3 3/6 6/2
25. **J.Eagle** (AUS) **& Miss B.Schett** (AUT) ....[11]
26. M.Hill (AUS) & Miss C.M.Vis (NED) ....
 — J.Eagle & Miss B.Schett [11] 6/2 4/6 6/2
27. D.Orsanic (ARG) & Mrs M.Vento-Kabchi (VEN) ....
28. T.Cibulec (CZE) & Miss E.Martincova (CZE) ....
 — D.Orsanic & Mrs M.Vento-Kabchi 6/4 6/4
 — J.Eagle & Miss B.Schett [11] ....6/3 7/6(2)
29. P.Haarhuis (NED) & Miss M.Oremans (NED) ....
30. D.Vacek (CZE) & Miss T.Poutchek (BLR) ....
 — P.Haarhuis & Miss M.Oremans ....7/6(3) 6/3
31. K.Braasch (GER) & Miss B.Rittner (GER) ....
32. **L.Paes** (IND) **& Miss L.M.Raymond** (USA) ....[5]
 — L.Paes & Miss L.M.Raymond [5] 6/2 3/6 9/7
 — L.Paes & Miss L.M.Raymond [5] 4/6 7/5 6/3
 — L.Paes & Miss L.M.Raymond [5] ....w/o
 — K.Ullyett & Miss D.Hantuchova [4] ....7/6(4) 4/6 6/4
33. **J.Bjorkman** (SWE) **& Miss A.Kournikova** (RUS) ......[7]
34. M.Barnard (RSA) & Miss K.Boogert (NED) ....
 — J.Bjorkman & Miss A.Kournikova [7] ....6/3 6/7(5) 6/4
35. J.Kerr (AUS) & Miss A.Van Exel (NED) ....
36. T.A.Woodbridge (AUS) & Miss M.Navratilova (USA) ......
 — T.A.Woodbridge & Miss M.Navratilova 4/6 6/3 9/7
 — J.Bjorkman & Miss A.Kournikova [7] 3/6 6/4 6/2
37. A.Olhovskiy (RUS) & Miss E.Tatarkova (UKR) ....
38. P.Pala (CZE) & Miss D.Bedanova (CZE) ....
 — P.Pala & Miss D.Bedanova 7/5 6/2
 — J.Bjorkman & Miss A.Kournikova [7] 7/5 6/4
39. A.Kratzmann (AUS) & Miss T.Musgrave (AUS) ....
40. **G.Etlis** (ARG) **& Miss P.Suarez** (ARG) ....[9]
 — A.Kratzmann & Miss T.Musgrave ....2/6 7/6(2) 6/4
 — A.Kratzmann & Miss T.Musgrave ....Ret'd
41. **M.Damm** (CZE) **& Miss K.Hrdlickova** (CZE) ....[15]
42. L.Arnold (ARG) & Mrs R.Neffa-De Los Rios (PAR) ....
 — M.Damm & Miss K.Hrdlickova [15] 6/1 6/1
43. J.Tarango (USA) & Miss N.Zvereva (BLR) ....
44. T.Shimada (JPN) & Miss R.Fujiwara (JPN) ....
 — T.Shimada & Miss R.Fujiwara 6/3 6/4
 — T.Shimada & Miss R.Fujiwara 6/2 6/1
45. D.Bowen (USA) & Miss R.Hiraki (JPN) ....
46. D.Macpherson (AUS) & Miss K.Schlukebir (USA) ....
 — D.Macpherson & Miss K.Schlukebir 6/4 6/4
 — M.Bhupathi & Miss E.Likhovtseva [3] 6/2 7/5
47. S.Stolle (AUS) & Miss R.McQuillan (AUS) ....
48. **M.Bhupathi** (IND) **& Miss E.Likhovtseva** (RUS) .....[3]
 — M.Bhupathi & Miss E.Likhovtseva [3] 6/3 6/4
 — M.Bhupathi & Miss E.Likhovtseva [3] 7/5 6/4
 — M.Bhupathi & Miss E.Likhovtseva [3] 6/4 6/2
49. **M.Bryan** (USA) **& Mrs L.Huber** (RSA) ....[6]
50. L.Friedl (CZE) & Miss T.Krizan (SLO) ....
 — M.Bryan & Mrs L.Huber [6] 6/2 6/4
51. T.Vanhoudt (BEL) & Miss A.Fusai (FRA) ....
52. R.Leach (USA) & Miss L.McShea (USA) ....
 — R.Leach & Miss L.McShea ....6/4 7/6(5)
 — M.Bryan & Mrs L.Huber [6] 6/3 6/4
53. N.Healey (AUS) & Miss A.Spears (USA) ....
54. T.Perry (AUS) & Miss A.Augustus (USA) ....
 — N.Healey & Miss A.Spears 4/6 6/4 6/2
 — B.Bryan & Miss K.Srebotnik [10] 3/6 6/2 6/3
(W)55. B.Cowan (GBR) & Miss V.E.Davies (GBR) ....
56. **B.Bryan** (USA) **& Miss K.Srebotnik** (SLO) ....[10]
 — B.Bryan & Miss K.Srebotnik [10] 6/1 6/1
 — B.Bryan & Miss K.Srebotnik [10] 6/4 6/4
 — B.Bryan & Miss K.Srebotnik [10] 3/6 6/2 6/3
57. **B.MacPhie** (USA) **& Miss A.J.Coetzer** (RSA) ....[13]
58. O.Fukarek (CZE) & Miss J.Husarova (SVK) ....
 — B.MacPhie & Miss A.J.Coetzer [13] 6/2 6/3
59. J-L.De Jager (RSA) & Miss K.Grant (RSA) ....
60. M.Rodriguez (ARG) & Miss S.Reeves (USA) ....
 — M.Rodriguez & Miss S.Reeves ....6/7(7) 6/2 9/7
 — B.MacPhie & Miss A.J.Coetzer [13] ....7/6(3) 4/6 8/6
61. S.Aspelin (SWE) & Miss N.De Villiers (RSA) ....
62. A.Kitinov (MKD) & Miss M.Matevzic (SLO) ....
 — S.Aspelin & Miss N.De Villiers ....4/6 7/6(4) 6/4
 — D.Johnson & Mrs K.Po-Messerli [2] 7/5 6/3
63. L.Lobo (ARG) & Miss L.Montalvo (ARG) ....
64. **D.Johnson** (USA) **& Mrs K.Po-Messerli** (USA) ....[2]
 — D.Johnson & Mrs K.Po-Messerli [2] 7/5 6/3
 — D.Johnson & Mrs K.Po-Messerli [2] ....7/6(4) 6/3

Third Round / Quarter-Final results:
- R.Koenig & Miss E.S.H.Callens [16] ....6/2 7/6(7)
- K.Ullyett & Miss D.Hantuchova [4] ....6/4 1/6 6/1 (final line: 6/2 1/6 6/1)
- M.Bhupathi & Miss E.Likhovtseva [3] 6/4 6/2
- D.Johnson & Mrs K.Po-Messerli [2] 4/6 6/3 6/4

Semi-final:
- K.Ullyett & Miss D.Hantuchova [4] 6/4 1/6 6/3
- M.Bhupathi & Miss E.Likhovtseva [3] 6/4 1/6 6/3

Final:
- **M.Bhupathi & Miss E.Likhovtseva [3]** 6/2 1/6 6/1

Heavy type denotes seeded players. The figure in brackets against names denotes the order in which they have been seeded. (W) = Wild card. (Q) = Qualifier. (L) = Lucky loser.

The matches are the best of three sets

The winners become the holders, for the year only, of a Cup presented by The All England Lawn Tennis and Croquet Club. The winners receive miniature silver salvers. A silver medal is presented to each of the runners-up.

Holders: J. B. Fitzgerald and W. Masur

GROUP A

	J.B. Fitzgerald (AUS) and W. Masur (AUS)	H. Leconte (FRA) and M. Pernfors (SWE)	K. Curren (USA) and J. Kriek (USA)	J. Frana (ARG) and S. Zivojinovic (YUG)	WINS	LOSSES
J.B. Fitzgerald (AUS) and W. Masur (AUS)		7/6(2) 4/6 6/1 W	3/6 7/5 6/3 W	7/5 6/4 W	3	0
H. Leconte (FRA) and M. Pernfors (SWE)	6/7(2) 6/4 1/6 L		W/O L	W/O L	0	3
K. Curren (USA) and J. Kriek (USA)	6/3 5/7 3/6 L	W/O W		4/6 6/3 7/5 W	2	1
J. Frana (ARG) and S. Zivojinovic (YUG)	5/7 4/6 L	W/O W	6/4 3/6 5/7 L		1	2

Semi-final: J.B. Fitzgerald (AUS) and W. Masur (AUS)

GROUP B

	B. Gilbert (USA) and A. Jarryd (SWE)	P. Aldrich (RSA) and D. Visser (RSA)	S. Davis (USA) and D. Pate (USA)	L. Shiras (USA) and T. Wilkison (USA)	WINS	LOSSES
B. Gilbert (USA) and A. Jarryd (SWE)		4/6 4/6 L	4/6 4/6 L	6/2 6/4 W	1	2
P. Aldrich (RSA) and D. Visser (RSA)	6/4 6/4 W		4/6 4/6 L	7/6(5) 7/6(6) W	2	1
S. Davis (USA) and D. Pate (USA)	6/4 6/4 W	6/4 6/4 W		7/5 6/3 W	3	0
L. Shiras (USA) and T. Wilkison (USA)	2/6 4/6 L	6/7(5) 6/7(6) L	5/6 3/6 L		0	3

Semi-final: S. Davis (USA) and D. Pate (USA)

Final (top): S. Davis (USA) and D. Pate (USA) 6/4 3/6 6/3

GROUP C

	P. Galbraith (USA) and S. Melville (USA)	N. Broad (GBR) and P. Hand (GBR)	H. Guenthardt (SUI) and D. Rostagno (USA)	J. Grabb (USA) and J. Pugh (USA)	WINS	LOSSES
P. Galbraith (USA) and S. Melville (USA)		7/5 3/6 5/7 L	6/4 6/4 W	6/4 6/4 W	2	1
N. Broad (GBR) and P. Hand (GBR)	5/7 6/3 7/5 W		7/6(2) 6/4 W	6/3 6/4 W	3	0
H. Guenthardt (SUI) and D. Rostagno (USA)	4/6 4/6 L	6/7(2) 4/6 L		6/7(4) 3/6 L	0	3
J. Grabb (USA) and J. Pugh (USA)	4/6 4/6 L	3/6 4/6 L	7/6(4) 6/3 W		1	2

Semi-final: N. Broad (GBR) and P. Hand (GBR)

GROUP D

	S. Casal (ESP) and E. Sanchez (ESP)	M.J. Bates (GBR) and N.A. Fulwood (GBR)	G.W. Donnelly (USA) and L. Jensen (USA)	J. Nystrom (SWE) and M. Wilander (SWE)	WINS	LOSSES
S. Casal (ESP) and E. Sanchez (ESP)		6/7(0) 7/5 5/7 L	6/4 6/2 W	2/6 6/7(4) L	1	2
M.J. Bates (GBR) and N.A. Fulwood (GBR)	7/6(0) 5/7 7/5 W		7/6(1) 6/3 W	3/6 6/1 6/2 W	3	0
G.W. Donnelly (USA) and L. Jensen (USA)	4/6 2/6 L	6/7(1) 3/6 L		6/2 2/6 2/6 L	0	3
J. Nystrom (SWE) and M. Wilander (SWE)	6/2 7/6(4) W	6/3 1/6 2/6 L	2/6 6/2 6/2 W		2	1

Semi-final: M.J. Bates (GBR) and N.A. Fulwood (GBR)

Final (bottom): M.J. Bates (GBR) and N.A. Fulwood (GBR) 7/6(6) 6/3

FINAL: S. Davis (USA) and D. Pate (USA) 6/3 7/6(3)

This event is played on a 'round robin' basis. 16 invited pairs are divided into four groups and each pair in each group plays the others. The pairs winning most matches are the winners of their respective groups and play semi-final and final rounds as indicated above. If matches should be equal in any group, the head-to-head result between the two pairs with the same number of wins determines the winning pair of the group. Heavy type denotes seeded players. **The matches are the best of three sets.** The tie-break will operate at six games all in the first two sets.

The winners become the holders, for the year only, of a Cup presented by The All England Lawn Tennis and Croquet Club. The winners receive miniature silver salvers. A silver medal is presented to each of the runners-up.

Holders: P. B. McNamara and P. F. McNamee

First Round	Quarter-Finals	Semi-Finals	Final
1. **P.B.McNamara** (AUS) & **P.F.McNamee** (AUS) .... [1]			
2. P.Slozil (CZE) & T.Smid (CZE)	P.B.McNamara & P.F.McNamee [1] — 6/2 6/0		
3. A.Amritraj (IND) & V.Amritraj (IND)		P.B.McNamara & P.F.McNamee [1] — 7/6(3) 7/6(5)	
4. B.E.Gottfried (USA) & T.R.Gullikson (USA)	B.E.Gottfried & T.R.Gullikson — 7/5 7/5		
5. **P.Fleming** (USA) & **A.A.Mayer** (USA) .... [3]			P.Fleming & A.A.Mayer [3] — 6/3 6/4
6. I.Nastase (ROM) & T.S.Okker (NED)	P.Fleming & A.A.Mayer [3] — 6/4 6/2		
7. R.L.Case (AUS) & G.Masters (AUS)		P.Fleming & A.A.Mayer [3] — 7/5 6/4	
8. J.W.Feaver (GBR) & J.M.Lloyd (GBR)	R.L.Case & G.Masters — 4/6 6/1 8/6		
9. J.D.Newcombe (AUS) & R.Tanner (USA)			C.Dowdeswell & C.J.Mottram [2] — 7/5 6/4
10. R.C.Lutz (USA) & S.R.Smith (USA)	R.C.Lutz & S.R.Smith — 4/6 6/3 6/3		
11. O.K.Davidson (AUS) & .A.Stone (AUS)		M.Bahrami & G.Mayer [4] — 6/3 7/5	
12. **M.Bahrami** (IRI) & **G.Mayer** (USA) .... [4]	M.Bahrami & G.Mayer [4] — 6/4 6/4		
13. M.C.Riessen (USA) & S.E.Stewart (USA)			C.Dowdeswell & C.J.Mottram [2] — 6/4 3/6 6/1
14. J.G.Alexander (AUS) & P.Dent (AUS)	J.G.Alexander & P.Dent — 6/4 6/2		
15. M.R.Edmondson (AUS) & R.J.Frawley (AUS)		C.Dowdeswell & C.J.Mottram [2] — 6/4 6/2	
16. **C.Dowdeswell** (GBR) & **C.J.Mottram** (GBR) ...... [2]	C.Dowdeswell & C.J.Mottram [2] — 6/3 6/3		

Heavy type denotes seeded players. The figure in brackets against names denotes the order in which they have been seeded. **The matches are the best of three sets.** The tie-break will operate at six games all in the first two sets.

THE 35 AND OVER LADIES' INVITATION DOUBLES

The winners become the holders, for the year only, of a Cup presented by The All England Lawn Tennis and Croquet Club. The winners receive miniature Cups. A silver medal is presented to each of the runners-up.

Holders: Miss I. Kloss and Mrs R. Nideffer

GROUP A	Miss J.A. Salmon (GBR) and Miss W.M. Turnbull (AUS)	Mrs K. Rinaldi (USA) and Miss S.V. Wade (GBR)	Miss A.E. Hobbs (GBR) and Miss C. Lindqvist (SWE)	Miss M. Jausovec (SLO) and Mrs G. Magers (USA)	WINS	LOSSES	FINAL
Miss J.A. Salmon (GBR) and Miss W.M. Turnbull (AUS)		5/7 1/6 L	2/6 2/6 L	6/7(3) 6/4 1/6 L	0	3	
Mrs K. Rinaldi (USA) and Miss S.V. Wade (GBR)	7/5 6/1 W		6/4 6/4 W	3/6 3/6 L	2	1	
Miss A.E. Hobbs (GBR) and Miss C. Lindqvist (SWE)	6/2 6/2 W	4/6 4/6 L		3/6 4/6 L	1	2	
Miss M. Jausovec (SLO) and Mrs G. Magers (USA)	7/6(3) 4/6 6/1 W	6/3 6/3 W	6/3 6/4 W		3	0	

Miss M. Jausovec (SLO) and Mrs G. Magers (USA)

GROUP B	Mrs R.D. Nideffer (RSA) and Miss H. Sukova (CZE)	Miss R. Casals (USA) and Miss S.L. Collins (USA)	Miss I. Kloss (RSA) and Miss H. Mandlikova (AUS)	Miss J.M. Durie (GBR) and Miss Y. Vermaak (RSA)	WINS	LOSSES	FINAL
Mrs R.D. Nideffer (RSA) and Miss H. Sukova (CZE)		6/1 7/5 W	6/1 6/1 W	6/2 6/1 W	3	0	
Miss R. Casals (USA) and Miss S.L. Collins (USA)	1/6 5/7 L		2/6 2/6 L	6/4 4/6 4/6 L	0	3	
Miss I. Kloss (RSA) and Miss H. Mandlikova (AUS)	1/6 1/6 L	6/2 6/2 W		6/3 6/3 W	2	1	
Miss J.M. Durie (GBR) and Miss Y. Vermaak (RSA)	2/6 1/6 L	4/6 6/4 6/4 W	3/6 3/6 L		1	2	

Mrs R.D. Nideffer (RSA) and Miss H. Sukova (CZE)

FINAL: Miss M. Jausovec (SLO) and Mrs G. Magers (USA) 6/3 6/3

This event is played on a 'round robin' basis. Eight invited pairs are divided into two groups and each pair in each group plays the others. The pairs winning most matches are the winners of their respective groups and play a final round as indicated above. If matches should be equal in any group, the head-to-head result between the two pairs with the same number of wins determines the winning pair of the group.

Heavy type denotes seeded players.

The matches are the best of three sets. The tie-break will operate at six games all in the first two sets.

ALPHABETICAL LIST – 35 AND OVER EVENTS

GENTLEMEN

Aldrich P. *(South Africa)*
Bates M.J. *(Great Britain)*
Broad N. *(Great Britain)*
Casal S. *(Spain)*
Curren K. *(USA)*
Davis S. *(USA)*
Donnelly G.W. *(USA)*
Fitzgerald J.B. *(Australia)*

Frana J. *(Argentina)*
Fulwood N.A. *(Great Britain)*
Galbraith P. *(USA)*
Gilbert B. *(USA)*
Grabb J. *(USA)*
Guenthardt H. *(Switzerland)*
Hand P. *(Great Britain)*
Jarryd A. *(Sweden)*

Jensen L. *(USA)*
Kriek J. *(USA)*
Leconte H. *(France)*
Masur W. *(Australia)*
Melville S. *(USA)*
Nystrom J. *(Sweden)*
Pate D. *(USA)*
Pernfors M. *(Sweden)*

Pugh J. *(USA)*
Rostagno D. *(USA)*
Sanchez E. *(Spain)*
Shiras L. *(USA)*
Visser D. *(South Africa)*
Wilander M. *(Sweden)*
Wilkison T. *(USA)*
Zivojinovic S. *(Yugoslavia)*

LADIES

Casals Miss R. *(USA)*
Collins Miss S.L. *(USA)*
Durie Miss J.M. *(Great Britain)*
Hobbs Miss A.E. *(Great Britain)*

Jausovec Miss M. *(Slovenia)*
Kloss Miss I. *(South Africa)*
Lindqvist Miss C. *(Sweden)*
Magers Mrs G. *(USA)*

Mandlikova Miss H. *(Australia)*
Nideffer Mrs R.D. *(South Africa)*
Rinaldi Mrs K. *(USA)*
Salmon Miss J.A *(Great Britain)*

Sukova Miss H. *(Czech Republic)*
Turnbull Miss W.M. *(Australia)*
Vermaak Miss Y. *(South Africa)*
Wade Miss S.V. *(Great Britain)*

ALPHABETICAL LIST – 45 AND OVER EVENT

GENTLEMEN

Alexander J.G. *(Australia)*
Amritraj A. *(India)*
Amritraj V. *(India)*
Bahrami M. *(Iran)*
Case R.L. *(Australia)*
Davidson O.K. *(Australia)*
Dent P. *(Australia)*
Dowdeswell C. *(Great Britain)*

Edmondson M.R. *(Australia)*
Feaver J.W. *(Great Britain)*
Fleming P. *(USA)*
Frawley R.J. *(Australia)*
Gottfried B.E. *(USA)*
Gullikson T.R. *(USA)*
Lloyd J.M. *(Great Britain)*
Lutz R.C. *(USA)*

Masters G. *(Australia)*
Mayer A.A. *(USA)*
Mayer G. *(USA)*
McNamara P.B. *(Australia)*
McNamee P.F. *(Australia)*
Mottram C.J. *(Great Britain)*
Nastase I. *(Romania)*
Newcombe J.D. *(Australia)*

Okker T.S. *(Netherlands)*
Riessen M.C. *(USA)*
Slozil P. *(Czech Republic)*
Smid T. *(Czech Republic)*
Smith S.R. *(USA)*
Stewart S.E. *(USA)*
Stone A. *(Australia)*
Tanner R. *(USA)*

For both the Boys' Singles *and* the Boys' Doubles Championships, the winners become the holders, for the year only, of a Cup presented by The All England Lawn Tennis and Croquet Club. The winners each receive a miniature Cup and the runners-up receive mementoes.

THE BOYS' SINGLES CHAMPIONSHIP

Holder: R. Valent

First Round

	No.	Player	Nation
	1.	**Wang Yeu-Tzuoo [1]**	(TPE)
	2.	Koning Michel	(NED)
(W)	3.	Smith Matthew	(GBR)
(L)	4.	Juska Andis	(LAT)
(W)	5.	Ram Rajeev	(USA)
	6.	Bonatto Alexandre	(BRA)
	7.	Kuseta Davor	(CRO)
	8.	**Tsonga Jo-Wilfried [16]**	(FRA)
	9.	**Baker Brian [12]**	(USA)
(Q)	10.	Durek Raphael	(AUS)
	11.	Brewer David	(GBR)
	12.	Westerhof Christopher	(RSA)
	13.	Kanev Yorden	(BUL)
	14.	Balazs Gyorgy	(HUN)
	15.	Dancevic Frank	(CAN)
	16.	**Reid Todd [5]**	(AUS)
	17.	**Baghdatis Marcos [4]**	(CYP)
	18.	Crawley Nicky	(GBR)
	19.	Kapun Anze	(SLO)
	20.	Bayer Markus	(GER)
	21.	Smeets Robert	(AUS)
(Q)	22.	Gabashvili Teimuraz	(RUS)
	23.	Stiegwardt Martin	(ECU)
	24.	**Montcourt Mathieu [13]**	(FRA)
	25.	**Darcis Steve [11]**	(BEL)
	26.	Lustig Daniel	(CZE)
	27.	Yim Robert	(USA)
	28.	Sottocorno Alberto	(BOL)
	29.	Loglo Komlavi	(TOG)
(W)	30.	Goodall Joshua	(GBR)
	31.	Przysiezny Michal	(POL)
	32.	**Felder Marcel [6]**	(URU)
	33.	**Ouahab Lamine [7]**	(ALG)
	34.	Ferreiro Franco	(BRA)
	35.	Haybittel Robert	(AUS)
(Q)	36.	Brown Dustin	(JAM)
(W)	37.	Murray Andrew	(GBR)
(Q)	38.	Skrypko Alexander	(BLR)
(Q)	39.	Sitak Artem	(RUS)
	40.	**Bogdanovic Alex [9]**	(GBR)
	41.	**Sela Dudi [14]**	(ISR)
	42.	Gregorc Luka	(SLO)
(Q)	43.	Ruiz Antonio	(MEX)
(W)	44.	Searle Robert	(GBR)
	45.	Evans Brendon	(USA)
	46.	Henry Ryan	(AUS)
(Q)	47.	Evans Craig	(GBR)
	48.	**Morel Clement [3]**	(FRA)
	49.	**Petzschner Philipp [8]**	(GER)
	50.	Van Der Valk Bas	(NED)
	51.	Guccione Chris	(AUS)
	52.	Cohen Josh	(USA)
	53.	Tecau Horia	(ROM)
(W)	54.	Thomas Guy	(GBR)
(Q)	55.	Mergea Florin	(ROM)
	56.	**Vilarrubi Martin [10]**	(URU)
	57.	**Berdych Tomas [15]**	(CZE)
	58.	Soeda Go	(JPN)
	59.	Liu Tai-Wei	(TPE)
	60.	Ryderstedt Michael	(SWE)
	61.	Kwon Chris	(USA)
(W)	62.	Hutchins Ross	(GBR)
(W)	63.	Nadal-Parera Rafael	(ESP)
	64.	**Dabul Brian [2]**	(ARG)

Second Round

- M.Koning 6/4 6/4
- M.Smith 6/2 7/6(6)
- R.Ram 7/6(0) 6/1
- **J.Tsonga [16]** 7/5 7/6(6)
- R.Durek 6/7(4) 7/5 7/5
- D.Brewer 3/6 7/6(1) 6/2
- Y.Kanev 6/4 6/2
- **T.Reid [5]** 6/1 5/7 6/0
- **M.Baghdatis [4]** 6/4 7/6(5)
- M.Bayer 6/2 7/5
- R.Smeets 3/6 7/6(4) 6/3
- **M.Montcourt [13]** 6/0 6/3
- **S.Darcis [11]** 6/3 6/4
- R.Yim 7/6(4) 3/6 6/4
- J.Goodall 2/6 7/6(5) 6/4
- **M.Felder [6]** 6/1 7/5
- **L.Ouahab [7]** 6/7(3) 6/3 6/2
- D.Brown 6/4 6/4
- A.Skrypko 7/6(5) 4/6 6/4
- **A.Bogdanovic [9]** 6/0 6/0
- L.Gregorc 1/6 6/4 6/1
- A.Ruiz 6/3 6/4
- R.Henry 7/6(4) 6/0
- **C.Morel [3]** 7/6(2) 3/6 6/3
- **P.Petzschner [8]** 6/4 7/5
- C.Guccione 6/1 6/3
- G.Thomas 7/6(7) 6/2
- F.Mergea 6/3 6/3
- **T.Berdych [15]** 6/4 6/2
- M.Ryderstedt 6/1 6/4
- C.Kwon 7/5 6/1
- R.Nadal-Parera 5/7 6/4 6/2

Third Round

- M.Koning 7/6(2) 7/6(1)
- **J.Tsonga [16]** 7/6(5) 6/4
- D.Brewer 6/4 6/4
- **T.Reid [5]** 6/1 6/1
- M.Bayer 6/2 6/4
- **M.Montcourt [13]** 6/2 6/3
- **S.Darcis [11]** 6/1 6/3
- J.Goodall 3/6 6/4 6/4
- **L.Ouahab [7]** 3/6 6/4 6/3
- A.Skrypko 7/6(5) 7/6(4)
- L.Gregorc 6/2 6/4
- R.Henry 7/5 6/7(3) 26/24
- **P.Petzschner [8]** 7/6(4) 7/6(4)
- G.Thomas 7/6(5) 6/4
- M.Ryderstedt 6/4 5/7 8/6
- R.Nadal-Parera 6/4 6/0

Quarter-Finals

- M.Koning 3/6 6/3 8/6
- **T.Reid [5]** 7/6(7) 6/2
- **M.Montcourt [13]** 6/2 4/6 9/7
- **S.Darcis [11]** 6/3 6/2
- **L.Ouahab [7]** 7/6(4) 6/1
- L.Gregorc 6/4 3/6 6/1
- **P.Petzschner [8]** 6/4 7/5
- R.Nadal-Parera 6/3 6/0

Semi-Finals

- **T.Reid [5]** 6/3 3/6 6/1
- **S.Darcis [11]** 6/4 2/6 6/4
- **L.Ouahab [7]** 3/6 6/4 6/1
- R.Nadal-Parera 2/6 6/3 6/4

Final

- **T.Reid [5]** 3/6 6/2 6/2
- **L.Ouahab [7]** 6/3 7/5

Winner: T.Reid [5] 7/6(5) 6/4

THE BOYS' DOUBLES CHAMPIONSHIP

Holders: F. Dancevic and G. Lapentti

First Round

1. **M.Bayer** (GER) **& P.Petzschner** (GER) [1]
2. T.Burn (GBR) & M.Lowe (GBR)
3. D.Brewer (GBR) & A.Murray (GBR)
4. S.Saengsuwarn (THA) & S.Shimizu (JPN)
5. Y.Kanev (BUL) & K.Loglo (TOG)
6. F.Mergea (ROM) & H.Tecau (ROM)
7. J.Cohen (USA) & D.Kuseta (CRO)
8. **T.Berdych** (CZE) **& S.Darcis** (BEL) [7]
9. **M.Koning** (NED) **& B.Van Der Valk** (NED) [4]
10. A.Bogdanovic (GBR) & B.Jelovac (GBR)
11. A.Ruiz (MEX) & A.Skrypko (BLR)
12. R.Haybittel (AUS) & R.Smeets (AUS)
13. R.Durek (AUS) & T.Gabashvili (RUS)
14. D.Brown (JAM) & A.Sottocorno (BOL)
15. J.Goodall (GBR) & A.Miotto (GBR)
16. **S.Amritraj** (USA) **& L.Ouahab** (ALG) [8]
17. **M.Felder** (URU) **& M.Vilarrubi** (URU) [5]
18. N.Crawley (GBR) & C.Evans (GBR)
19. R.Hutchins (GBR) & G.Thomas (GBR)
20. B.Baker (USA) & R.Ram (USA)
21. C.Kwon (USA) & M.Ryderstedt (SWE)
22. A.Kapun (SLO) & D.Lustig (CZE)
23. T-W.Liu (TPE) & G.Soeda (JPN)
24. **A.Feeney** (AUS) **& C.Guccione** (AUS) [3]
25. **M.Stiegwardt** (ECU) **& C.Westerhof** (RSA) [6]
26. B.Hung (HKG) & H-T.Yu (HKG)
27. R.Searle (GBR) & M.Smith (GBR)
28. A.Bonatto (BRA) & F.Ferreiro (BRA)
29. B.Rufer (SUI) & A.Sitak (RUS)
30. G.Balazs (HUN) & M.Przysiezny (POL)
31. A.Juska (LAT) & R.Yim (USA)
32. **R.Henry** (AUS) **& T.Reid** (AUS) [2]

Second Round

- **M.Bayer & P.Petzschner [1]** 6/4 7/6(2)
- D.Brewer & A.Murray 6/7(5) 6/4 6/1
- F.Mergea & H.Tecau 6/7(4) 6/4 8/6
- **T.Berdych & S.Darcis [7]** w/o
- **M.Koning & B.Van Der Valk [4]** 7/6(6) 6/4
- R.Haybittel & R.Smeets 6/4 6/3
- R.Durek & T.Gabashvili 6/7(5) 6/3 8/6
- **S.Amritraj & L.Ouahab [8]** 6/3 6/4
- **M.Felder & M.Vilarrubi [5]** 6/1 3/6 6/2
- B.Baker & R.Ram 7/5 7/6(5)
- C.Kwon & M.Ryderstedt w/o
- T-W.Liu & G.Soeda 6/3 6/4
- **M.Stiegwardt & C.Westerhof [6]** 6/3 7/6(2)
- R.Searle & M.Smith 6/3 6/3
- B.Rufer & A.Sitak w/o
- **R.Henry & T.Reid [2]** 6/3 6/3

Quarter-Finals

- **M.Bayer & P.Petzschner [1]** 6/4 6/4
- F.Mergea & H.Tecau Ret'd
- R.Haybittel & R.Smeets 6/3 6/7(2) 8/6
- **S.Amritraj & L.Ouahab [8]** 6/1 6/4
- B.Baker & R.Ram 6/3 6/2
- T-W.Liu & G.Soeda 4/6 6/3 8/6
- R.Searle & M.Smith 7/5 6/2
- **R.Henry & T.Reid [2]** w/o

Semi-Finals

- F.Mergea & H.Tecau 6/3 7/6(6)
- R.Haybittel & R.Smeets 5/7 6/3 11/9
- B.Baker & R.Ram 7/5 6/2
- R.Searle & M.Smith 6/3 6/4

Final

- F.Mergea & H.Tecau 6/1 7/6(2)
- B.Baker & R.Ram 6/4 6/4

Winners: F.Mergea & H.Tecau 6/4 4/6 6/4

Heavy type denotes seeded players. The figure in brackets against names denotes the order in which they have been seeded. (W) = Wild card. (Q) = Qualifier. (L) = Lucky loser.

The matches are the best of three sets

THE GIRLS' SINGLES CHAMPIONSHIP

Holder: Miss A. Widjaja

	First Round	Second Round	Third Round	Quarter-Finals	Semi-Finals	Final
(L)	1. Tavares Marina.........................(BRA)	Miss A.Liu.....................6/2 6/2				
	2. Liu Amber.................................(USA)		Miss D.Casanova			
	3. Anderson Kelly..........................(RSA)	Miss D.Casanova 6/2 6/3	.................6/2 4/6 6/2			
	4. Casanova Daniela......................(SUI)			Miss T.Golovin [16]		
	5. Clijsters Elke............................(BEL)	Miss A.Hawkins...........6/7(5) 6/1 6/0				
(W)	6. Hawkins Anna...........................(GBR)		Miss T.Golovin [16]			
	7. Mirza Sania..............................(IND)	Miss T.Golovin [16]........6/4 6/1	.................6/2 6/1	.................6/0 6/2		
	8. Golovin Tatiana [16]..................(FRA)				Miss T.Golovin [16]	
	9. Bastrikova Anna [12].................(RUS)	Miss A.Bastrikova [12].....6/1 6/2			.................6/2 7/6(8)	
(W)	10. South Melanie............................(GBR)		Miss A.Bastrikova [12]			
(Q)	11. Tanaka Shiho............................(JPN)	Miss S.Tanaka...............6/2 6/3	.................6/3 6/0			
	12. Miseviciute Aurelija...................(LTU)			Miss A.Bastrikova [12]		
	13. Israilova Ivanna........................(UZB)	Miss I.Israilova...............3/6 6/4 6/3				
(W)	14. Mueller Alexandra.....................(GBR)		Miss I.Israilova	.................6/4 6/2		
	15. Hlavackova Andrea....................(CZE)	Miss A-L.Groenefeld [6]....7/5 6/3	.................7/6(4) 4/6 6/1			
	16. Groenefeld Anna-Lena [6]..........(GER)					Miss V.Douchevina [8]
	17. Strycova Barbora [3].................(CZE)	Miss B.Strycova [3]........6/3 5/7 6/0				.................6/3 6/1
	18. Babos Zsuzsanna......................(HUN)		Miss E.Linetskaya			
(Q)	19. Kuryanovich Iryna.....................(BLR)	Miss E.Linetskaya...........6/1 7/6(5)	.................6/3 6/4			
	20. Linetskaya Eugenia....................(RUS)			Miss E.Linetskaya		
(Q)	21. Rankin Rebecca........................(USA)	Miss T.Welford...............7/6(3) 6/1				
(Q)	22. Welford Tiffany.........................(AUS)		Miss A.Baker [14]	.................6/3 6/4		
	23. Lyubtsova Oxana.......................(UKR)	Miss A.Baker [14]...........7/5 6/3	.................6/1 4/6 6/1			
	24. Baker Ally [14].........................(USA)				Miss V.Douchevina [8]	
	25. Klepac Andreja [11]...................(SLO)	Miss A.Klepac................7/6(5) 6/1			.................6/1 4/6 6/1	
	26. Correa Mariana.........................(ECU)		Miss K.Czafikova			
	27. Czafikova Kristina.....................(SVK)	Miss K.Czafikova...........2/6 6/3 8/6	.................6/3 6/3			
(W)	28. Grady Hannah...........................(GBR)			Miss V.Douchevina [8]		
	29. Tamaela Elise...........................(NED)	Miss Y.Sema.........7/6(5) 6/7(3) 8/6				
(Q)	30. Sema Yurika.............................(JPN)		Miss V.Douchevina [8]	.................6/2 6/3		
	31. Rao Sunitha.............................(USA)	Miss V.Douchevina [8]......6/3 6/4	.................6/2 6/2			
	32. Douchevina Vera [8]..................(RUS)					
	33. Sharapova Maria [7]..................(RUS)	Miss M.Sharapova [7]......3/6 6/2 6/2				
	34. Gajdosova Jarmila.....................(SVK)		Miss M.Sharapova [7]			
(W)	35. Khalifa Amany..........................(EGY)	Miss K.O'Brien................6/4 6/4	.................6/1 6/1			
(W)	36. O'Brien Katie............................(GBR)			Miss M.Sharapova [7]		
(L)	37. Ivanov Darya............................(AUS)	Miss J.Jackson...............7/5 4/6 6/4				
	38. Jackson Jamea.........................(USA)		Miss S.Bauer [9]	.................7/5 6/3		
(Q)	39. Terblanche Tarryn.....................(RSA)	Miss S.Bauer [9]............6/2 6/1	.................7/6(4) 6/3			
	40. Bauer Silvana [9]......................(NED)				Miss M.Sharapova [7]	
	41. Avants Cory Ann [15].................(USA)	Miss C.Avants [15]..........7/5 6/0			.................6/0 6/2	
(L)	42. Vialiamovskaia Marina................(RUS)		Miss C.Avants [15]			
(W)	43. Webley-Smith Emily...................(GBR)	Miss E.Webley-Smith.......6/2 6/2	.................6/3 6/0			
	44. Laosirichon Pichaya...................(THA)			Miss C.Avants [15]		
	45. Teller Petra.............................(HUN)	Miss K.Blocker.........6/2 6/7(7) 8/6				
	46. Blocker Katja............................(GER)		Miss E.Birnerova [4]	.................4/6 6/4 6/3		
(Q)	47. Laine Emma.............................(FIN)	Miss E.Birnerova [4]........7/5 1/6 9/7	.................6/4 6/2			
	48. Birnerova Eva [4]......................(CZE)					Miss V.Douchevina [8]
	49. Cetkovska Petra [5]...................(CZE)	Miss C.Gullickson...........6/2 5/7 6/1				.................4/6 6/1 6/2
	50. Gullickson Carly.......................(USA)		Miss C.Gullickson			
	51. Zawacki Tory............................(USA)	Miss T.Zawacki...............6/2 1/6 6/2	.................7/6(7) 6/0			
(W)	52. Flavell Francesca.......................(GBR)			Miss M.Kirilenko [10]		
	53. Ivanovic Ana............................(YUG)	Miss N.Ozegovic......3/6 7/6(3) 6/3				
	54. Ozegovic Nika...........................(CRO)		Miss M.Kirilenko [10]	.................3/6 6/4 6/3		
	55. Devidze Salome.........................(GEO)	Miss M.Kirilenko [10].......6/3 6/0	.................6/2 6/2			
	56. Kirilenko Maria [10]...................(RUS)				Miss M.Kirilenko [10]	
	57. Stosur Samantha [13].................(AUS)	Miss R.Oprandi.........6/3 4/3 Ret'd			.................4/6 4/4	
	58. Oprandi Romina.........................(SUI)		Miss L.Smolenakova			
	59. Domachowska Marta...................(POL)	Miss L.Smolenakova.........6/4 6/1	.................6/0 6/4			
	60. Smolenakova Linda.....................(SVK)			Miss L.Smolenakova		
	61. Robinson Shadisha.....................(USA)	Miss S.Robinson..............6/1 6/4				
	62. Sourkova Anastassia..................(RUS)		Miss A.Barnes	.................7/6(9) 7/5		
(Q)	63. Barnes Alice.............................(GBR)	Miss A.Barnes.................6/4 6/3	.................6/1 6/3			
	64. Hsieh Su-Wei [2].......................(TPE)					

THE GIRLS' DOUBLES CHAMPIONSHIP

Holders: Miss G. Dulko and Miss A. Harkleroad

	First Round	Second Round	Quarter-Finals	Semi-Finals	Final
	1. Miss E.Clijsters (BEL) & Miss B.Strycova (CZE) ......[1]	Miss E.Clijsters & Miss B.Strycova [1]............6/0 6/2	Miss E.Clijsters & Miss B.Strycova [1]		
	2. Miss K.O'Brien (GBR) & Miss M.South (GBR)				
(W)	3. Miss R.Rankin (GBR) & Miss L.Stanciute (LTU)	Miss K.Anderson & Miss P.Laosirichon 6/3 6/3	.................6/1 6/1	Miss E.Clijsters & Miss B.Strycova [1]	
	4. Miss K.Anderson (RSA) & Miss P.Laosirichon (THA) ...				
	5. Miss Z.Babos (HUN) & Miss S.Rao (USA)	Miss Z.Babos & Miss S.Rao.........................6/2 6/2	Miss M.Falcon & Miss S-W.Hsieh [8]	.................7/6(3) 6/7(5) 6/4	
	6. Miss M.Correa (ECU) & Miss T.Zawacki (USA)				
	7. Miss Y.Sema (JPN) & Miss M.Tavares (JPN)	Miss M.Falcon & Miss S-W.Hsieh [8]...............6/4 6/2	.................6/3 7/6(8)		
	8. Miss M.Falcon (USA) & Miss S-W.Hsieh (TPE) ......[8]				Miss E.Clijsters & Miss B.Strycova [1]
	9. Miss S.Bauer (NED) & Miss E.Tamaela (NED) ......[3]	Miss S.Bauer & Miss E.Tamaela [3] 6/4 6/1	Miss S.Bauer & Miss E.Tamaela [3]		.................6/4 6/3
	10. Miss A.Barnes (GBR) & Miss E.Webley-Smith (GBR) ..				
	11. Miss A.Klepac (SLO) & Miss S.Mirza (IND)	Miss D.Ivanov & Miss T.Welford ....3/6 7/6(4) 7/5	.................6/2 6/2	Miss J.Gajdosova & Miss A.Hlavackova [5]	
	12. Miss D.Ivanov (AUS) & Miss T.Welford (AUS)				
	13. Miss T.Terblanche (RSA) & Miss D.Van Boekel (NED)	Miss T.Terblanche & Miss D.Van Boekel ....w/o	Miss J.Gajdosova & Miss A.Hlavackova [5]	.................7/6(5) 6/2	
	14. Miss C.Dellacqua (AUS) & Miss S.Stosur (AUS)				
	15. Miss C.Gullickson (USA) & Miss J.Jackson (USA)	Miss J.Gajdosova & Miss A.Hlavackova [5]..6/2 7/6(4)	.................w/o		
	16. Miss J.Gajdosova (SVK) & Miss A.Hlavackova (CZE)..[5]				Miss E.Clijsters & Miss B.Strycova [1]
	17. Miss S.Devidze (GEO) & Miss E.Linetskaya (RUS) .[7]	Miss R.Oprandi & Miss M.Tavares ....w/o	Miss R.Oprandi & Miss M.Tavares		.................6/4 5/7 8/6
	18. Miss R.Oprandi (SUI) & Miss M.Tavares (BRA)				
	19. Miss A.Khalifa (EGY) & Miss O.Lyubtsova (UKR)	Miss C.Avants & Miss S.Robinson 6/1 6/3	.................w/o	Miss R.Oprandi & Miss M.Tavares	
	20. Miss C.Avants (USA) & Miss S.Robinson (USA)				
	21. Miss A.Sourkova (RUS) & Miss M.Vialiamovskaia (RUS)	Miss K.Blocker & Miss D.Casanova 6/4 6/4	Miss F.Flavell & Miss A.Hawkins	.................7/6(4) 6/4	
	22. Miss K.Blocker (GER) & Miss D.Casanova (SUI)				
	23. Miss F.Flavell (GBR) & Miss A.Hawkins (GBR)	Miss F.Flavell & Miss A.Hawkins ....w/o	.................4/5 Ret'd		
	24. Miss E.Birnerova (CZE) & Miss P.Cetkovska (CZE) .[4]				Miss A.Baker & Miss A-L.Groenefeld [2]
	25. Miss A.Bastrikova (RUS) & Miss V.Douchevina (RUS) ..[6]	Miss A.Bastrikova & Miss V.Douchevina [6] ....w/o	Miss A.Bastrikova & Miss V.Douchevina [6]		.................7/6(1) 6/4
	26. Miss A.Liu (USA) & Miss A.Miseviciute (LTU)				
	27. Miss M.Kirilenko (RUS) & Miss E.Laine (FIN)	Miss M.Kirilenko & Miss E.Laine 6/3 6/3	.................6/4 6/2	Miss A.Baker & Miss A-L.Groenefeld [2]	
	28. Miss H.Grady (GBR) & Miss A.Mueller (GBR)				
	29. Miss A.Ivanovic (YUG) & Miss N.Ozegovic (CRO)	Miss I.Israilova & Miss I.Kuryanovich 6/2 6/2	Miss A.Baker & Miss A-L.Groenefeld [2]	.................6/4 4/6 6/3	
	30. Miss I.Israilova (UZB) & Miss I.Kuryanovich (BLR)				
	31. Miss K.Czafikova (SVK) & Miss L.Smolenakova (SVK)	Miss A.Baker & Miss A-L.Groenefeld [2] 6/1 6/2	.................6/2 6/2		
	32. Miss A.Baker (USA) & Miss A-L.Groenefeld (GER) [2]				

Heavy type denotes seeded players. The figure in brackets against names denotes the order in which they have been seeded. (W) = Wild card. (Q) = Qualifier. (L) = Lucky loser.

The matches are the best of three sets

Year	Champion / Runner-up	Year	Champion / Runner-up	Year	Champion / Runner-up	Year	Champion / Runner-up	Year	Champion / Runner-up
1877	S. W. Gore / W. C. Marshall	1900	R. F. Doherty / S. H. Smith	1927	H. Cochet / J. Borotra	★ 1956	L. A. Hoad / K. R. Rosewall	1979	B. Borg / R. Tanner
1878	P. F. Hadow / S. W. Gore	1901	A. W. Gore / R. F. Doherty	1928	R. Lacoste / H. Cochet	1957	L. A. Hoad / A. J. Cooper	1980	B. Borg / J. P. McEnroe
★ 1879	J. T. Hartley / V. St. L. Goold	1902	H. L. Doherty / A. W. Gore	★ 1929	H. Cochet / J. Borotra	★ 1958	A. J. Cooper / N. A. Fraser	1981	J. P. McEnroe / B. Borg
1880	J. T. Hartley / H. F. Lawford	1903	H. L. Doherty / F. L. Riseley	1930	W. T. Tilden / W. Allison	★ 1959	A. Olmedo / R. Laver	1982	J. S. Connors / J. P. McEnroe
1881	W. Renshaw / J. T. Hartley	1904	H. L. Doherty / F. L. Riseley	★ 1931	S. B. Wood / F. X. Shields	★ 1960	N. A. Fraser / R. Laver	1983	J. P. McEnroe / C. J. Lewis
1882	W. Renshaw / E. Renshaw	1905	H. L. Doherty / N. E. Brookes	1932	H. E. Vines / H. W. Austin	1961	R. Laver / C. R. McKinley	1984	J. P. McEnroe / J. S. Connors
1883	W. Renshaw / E. Renshaw	1906	H. L. Doherty / F. L. Riseley	1933	J. H. Crawford / H. E. Vines	1962	R. Laver / M. F. Mulligan	1985	B. Becker / K. Curren
1884	W. Renshaw / H. F. Lawford	★ 1907	N. E. Brookes / A. W. Gore	1934	F. J. Perry / J. H. Crawford	★ 1963	C. R. McKinley / F. S. Stolle	1986	B. Becker / I. Lendl
1885	W. Renshaw / H. F. Lawford	★ 1908	A. W. Gore / H. Roper Barrett	1935	F. J. Perry / G. von Cramm	1964	R. Emerson / F. S. Stolle	1987	P. Cash / I. Lendl
1886	W. Renshaw / H. F. Lawford	1909	A. W. Gore / M. J. G. Ritchie	1936	F. J. Perry / G. von Cramm	1965	R. Emerson / F. S. Stolle	1988	S. Edberg / B. Becker
★ 1887	H. F. Lawford / E. Renshaw	1910	A. F. Wilding / A. W. Gore	★ 1937	J. D. Budge / G. von Cramm	1966	M. Santana / R. D. Ralston	1989	B. Becker / S. Edberg
1888	E. Renshaw / H. F. Lawford	1911	A. F. Wilding / H. Roper Barrett	1938	J. D. Budge / H. W. Austin	1967	J. D. Newcombe / W. P. Bungert	1990	S. Edberg / B. Becker
1889	W. Renshaw / E. Renshaw	1912	A. F. Wilding / A. W. Gore	★ 1939	R. L. Riggs / E. T. Cooke	1968	R. Laver / A. D. Roche	1991	M. Stich / B. Becker
1890	W. J. Hamilton / W. Renshaw	1913	A. F. Wilding / M. E. McLoughlin	★ 1946	Y. Petra / G. E. Brown	1969	R. Laver / J. D. Newcombe	1992	A. Agassi / G. Ivanisevic
★ 1891	W. Baddeley / J. Pim	1914	N. E. Brookes / A. F. Wilding	1947	J. Kramer / T. Brown	1970	J. D. Newcombe / K. R. Rosewall	1993	P. Sampras / J. Courier
1892	W. Baddeley / J. Pim	1919	G. L. Patterson / N. E. Brookes	★ 1948	R. Falkenburg / J. E. Bromwich	1971	J. D. Newcombe / S. R. Smith	1994	P. Sampras / G. Ivanisevic
1893	J. Pim / W. Baddeley	1920	W. T. Tilden / G. L. Patterson	1949	F. R. Schroeder / J. Drobny	★ 1972	S. R. Smith / I. Nastase	1995	P. Sampras / B. Becker
1894	J. Pim / W. Baddeley	1921	W. T. Tilden / B. I. C. Norton	★ 1950	B. Patty / F. A. Sedgman	★ 1973	J. Kodes / A. Metreveli	1996	R. Krajicek / M. Washington
★ 1895	W. Baddeley / W. V. Eaves	★†1922	G. L. Patterson / R. Lycett	1951	R. Savitt / K. McGregor	1974	J. S. Connors / K. R. Rosewall	1997	P. Sampras / C. Pioline
1896	H. S. Mahony / W. Baddeley	★ 1923	W. M. Johnston / F. T. Hunter	1952	F. A. Sedgman / J. Drobny	1975	A. R. Ashe / J. S. Connors	1998	P. Sampras / G. Ivanisevic
1897	R. F. Doherty / H. S. Mahony	★ 1924	J. Borotra / R. Lacoste	★ 1953	V. Seixas / K. Nielsen	1976	B. Borg / I. Nastase	1999	P. Sampras / A. Agassi
1898	R. F. Doherty / H. L. Doherty	1925	R. Lacoste / J. Borotra	1954	J. Drobny / K. R. Rosewall	1977	B. Borg / J. S. Connors	2000	P. Sampras / P. Rafter
1899	R. F. Doherty / A. W. Gore	★ 1926	J. Borotra / H. Kinsey	1955	T. Trabert / K. Nielsen	1978	B. Borg / J. S. Connors	2001	G. Ivanisevic / P. Rafter

NOTE: For the years 1913, 1914 and 1919-'23 inclusive the Championship Roll includes the 'World's Championships on Grass' granted to The Lawn Tennis Association by The International Lawn Tennis Federation. This title was then abolished and commencing in 1924 they became The Official Lawn Tennis Championships recognised by The International Lawn Tennis Federation. Prior to 1922 the holders in the singles events and the gentlemen's doubles did not compete in The Championships but met the winners of these events in the Challenge Rounds.
† Challenge Round abolished; holders subsequently played through.   *The holder did not defend the title.

Champions and Runners-up

Year	Champion / Runner-up	Year	Champion / Runner-up	Year	Champion / Runner-up
1884	Miss M. Watson / *Miss L. Watson*	1906	Miss D. K. Douglass / *Miss M. Sutton*	*1932	Mrs. F. S. Moody / *Miss H. H. Jacobs*
1885	Miss M. Watson / *Miss B. Bingley*	1907	Miss M. Sutton / *Mrs. Lambert Chambers*	1933	Mrs. F. S. Moody / *Miss D. E. Round*
1886	Miss B. Bingley / *Miss M. Watson*	*1908	Mrs. A. Sterry / *Miss A. M. Morton*	*1934	Miss D. E. Round / *Miss H. H. Jacobs*
1887	Miss L. Dod / *Miss B. Bingley*	*1909	Miss D. P. Boothby / *Miss A. M. Morton*	1935	Mrs. F. S. Moody / *Miss H. H. Jacobs*
1888	Miss L. Dod / *Mrs. G. W. Hillyard*	1910	Mrs. Lambert Chambers / *Miss D. P. Boothby*	*1936	Miss H. H. Jacobs / *Frau. S. Sperling*
*1889	Mrs. G. W. Hillyard / *Miss L. Rice*	1911	Mrs. Lambert Chambers / *Miss D. P. Boothby*	1937	Miss D. E. Round / *Miss J. Jedrzejowska*
*1890	Miss L. Rice / *Miss M. Jacks*	*1912	Mrs. D. R. Larcombe / *Mrs. A. Sterry*	*1938	Mrs. F. S. Moody / *Miss H. H. Jacobs*
*1891	Miss L. Dod / *Mrs. G. W. Hillyard*	*1913	Mrs. Lambert Chambers / *Mrs. R. J. McNair*	*1939	Miss A. Marble / *Miss K. E. Stammers*
1892	Miss L. Dod / *Mrs. G. W. Hillyard*	1914	Mrs. Lambert Chambers / *Mrs. D. R. Larcombe*	*1946	Miss P. Betz / *Miss L. Brough*
1893	Miss L. Dod / *Mrs. G. W. Hillyard*	1919	Mlle. S. Lenglen / *Mrs. Lambert Chambers*	*1947	Miss M. Osborne / *Miss D. Hart*
*1894	Mrs. G. W. Hillyard / *Miss E. L. Austin*	1920	Mlle. S. Lenglen / *Mrs. Lambert Chambers*	1948	Miss L. Brough / *Miss D. Hart*
*1895	Miss C. Cooper / *Miss H. Jackson*	1921	Mlle. S. Lenglen / *Miss E. Ryan*	1949	Miss L. Brough / *Mrs. W. du Pont*
1896	Miss C. Cooper / *Mrs. W. H. Pickering*	†1922	Mlle. S. Lenglen / *Mrs. F. Mallory*	1950	Miss L. Brough / *Mrs. W. du Pont*
1897	Mrs. G. W. Hillyard / *Miss C. Cooper*	1923	Mlle. S. Lenglen / *Miss K. McKane*	1951	Miss D. Hart / *Miss S. Fry*
*1898	Miss C. Cooper / *Miss L Martin*	1924	Miss K. McKane / *Miss H. Wills*	1952	Miss M. Connolly / *Miss L. Brough*
1899	Mrs. G. W. Hillyard / *Miss C. Cooper*	1925	Mlle. S. Lenglen / *Miss J. Fry*	1953	Miss M. Connolly / *Miss D. Hart*
1900	Mrs. G. W. Hillyard / *Miss C. Cooper*	1926	Mrs. L. A. Godfree / *Sta. L. de Alvarez*	1954	Miss M. Connolly / *Miss L. Brough*
1901	Mrs. A. Sterry / *Mrs. G. W. Hillyard*	1927	Miss H. Wills / *Sta. L. de Alvarez*	*1955	Miss L. Brough / *Mrs. J. G. Fleitz*
1902	Miss M. E. Robb / *Mrs. A. Sterry*	1928	Miss H. Wills / *Sta. L. de Alvarez*	1956	Miss S. Fry / *Miss A. Buxton*
*1903	Miss D. K. Douglass / *Miss E. W. Thomson*	1929	Miss H. Wills / *Miss H. H. Jacobs*	*1957	Miss A. Gibson / *Miss D. R. Hard*
1904	Miss D. K. Douglass / *Mrs. A. Sterry*	1930	Mrs. F. S. Moody / *Miss E. Ryan*	1958	Miss A. Gibson / *Miss A. Mortimer*
1905	Miss M. Sutton / *Miss D. K. Douglass*	*1931	Fraulein C. Aussem / *Fraulein H. Krahwinkel*		

Year	Champion / Runner-up	Year	Champion / Runner-up
*1959	Miss M. E. Bueno / *Miss D. R. Hard*	1980	Mrs. R. Cawley / *Mrs. J. M. Lloyd*
1960	Miss M. E. Bueno / *Miss S. Reynolds*	*1981	Mrs. J. M. Lloyd / *Miss H. Mandlikova*
*1961	Miss A. Mortimer / *Miss C. C. Truman*	1982	Miss M. Navratilova / *Mrs. J. M. Lloyd*
1962	Mrs. J. R. Susman / *Mrs. V. Sukova*	1983	Miss M. Navratilova / *Miss A. Jaeger*
*1963	Miss M. Smith / *Miss B. J. Moffitt*	1984	Miss M. Navratilova / *Mrs. J. M. Lloyd*
1964	Miss M. E. Bueno / *Miss M. Smith*	1985	Miss M. Navratilova / *Mrs. J. M. Lloyd*
1965	Miss M. Smith / *Miss M. E. Bueno*	1986	Miss M. Navratilova / *Miss H. Mandlikova*
1966	Mrs. L. W. King / *Miss M. E. Bueno*	1987	Miss M. Navratilova / *Miss S. Graf*
1967	Mrs. L. W. King / *Mrs. P. F. Jones*	1988	Miss S. Graf / *Miss M. Navratilova*
1968	Mrs. L. W. King / *Miss J. A. M. Tegart*	1989	Miss S. Graf / *Miss M. Navratilova*
1969	Mrs. P. F. Jones / *Mrs. L. W. King*	1990	Miss M. Navratilova / *Miss Z. Garrison*
*1970	Mrs. B. M. Court / *Mrs. L. W. King*	1991	Miss S. Graf / *Miss G. Sabatini*
1971	Miss E. F. Goolagong / *Mrs. B. M. Court*	1992	Miss S. Graf / *Miss M. Seles*
1972	Mrs. L. W. King / *Miss E. F. Goolagong*	1993	Miss S. Graf / *Miss J. Novotna*
1973	Mrs. L. W. King / *Miss C. M. Evert*	1994	Miss C. Martinez / *Miss M. Navratilova*
1974	Miss C. M. Evert / *Mrs. O. Morozova*	1995	Miss S. Graf / *Miss A. Sanchez Vicario*
1975	Mrs. L. W. King / *Mrs. R. Cawley*	1996	Miss S. Graf / *Miss A. Sanchez Vicario*
*1976	Miss C. M. Evert / *Mrs. R. Cawley*	*1997	Miss M. Hingis / *Miss J. Novotna*
1977	Miss S. V. Wade / *Miss B. F. Stove*	1998	Miss J. Novotna / *Miss N. Tauziat*
1978	Miss M. Navratilova / *Miss C. M. Evert*	1999	Miss L. A. Davenport / *Miss S. Graf*
1979	Miss M. Navratilova / *Mrs. J. M. Lloyd*	2000	Miss V. Williams / *Miss L. A. Davenport*
		2001	Miss V. Williams / *Miss J. Henin*

MAIDEN NAMES OF LADY CHAMPIONS

In the tables the following have been recorded in both married and single identities.

Mrs. R. Cawley ....Miss E. F. Goolagong	Mrs. G. W. Hillyard ....Miss B. Bingley	Mrs. F. S. Moody ....Miss H. Wills
Mrs. Lambert Chambers ....Miss D. K. Douglass	Mrs. P. F. Jones ....Miss A. S. Haydon	Mrs. O. Morozova ....Miss O. Morozova
Mrs. B. M. Court.....................Miss M. Smith	Mrs. L. W. King ....Miss B. J. Moffitt	Mrs. L. E. G. Price....................Miss S. Reynolds
Mrs. B. C. Covell.....................Miss P. L. Howkins	Mrs. M. R. King ....Miss P. E. Mudford	Mrs. G. E. Reid........................Miss K. Melville
Mrs. D. E. Dalton ....Miss J. A. M. Tegart	Mrs. D. R. Larcombe ....Miss E. W. Thomson	Mrs. P. D. Smylie ....Miss E. M. Sayers
Mrs. W. du Pont ....Miss M. Osborne	Mrs. J. M. Lloyd.......................Miss C. M. Evert	Frau. S. Sperling ....Fraulein H. Krahwinkel
Mrs. L. A. Godfree ....Miss K. McKane		Mrs. A. Sterry ....Miss C. Cooper
Mrs. H. F. Gourlay Cawley ....Miss H. F. Gourlay		Mrs. J. R. Susman ....Miss K. Hantze

GENTLEMEN'S DOUBLES

1879 L. R. Erskine and H. F. Lawford
F. Durant and G. E. Tabor
1880 W. Renshaw and E. Renshaw
O. E. Woodhouse and C. J. Cole
1881 W. Renshaw and E. Renshaw
W. J. Down and H. Vaughan
1882 J. T. Hartley and R. T. Richardson
J. G. Horn and C. B. Russell
1883 C. W. Grinstead and C. E. Welldon
C. B. Russell and R. T. Milford
1884 W. Renshaw and E. Renshaw
E. W. Lewis and E. L. Williams
1885 W. Renshaw and E. Renshaw
C. E. Farrer and A. J. Stanley
1886 W. Renshaw and E. Renshaw
C. E. Farrer and A. J. Stanley
1887 P. Bowes-Lyon and H. W. W. Wilberforce
J. H. Crispe and E. Barratt Smith
1888 W. Renshaw and E. Renshaw
P. Bowes-Lyon and H. W. W. Wilberforce
1889 W. Renshaw and E. Renshaw
E. W. Lewis and G. W. Hillyard
1890 J. Pim and F. O. Stoker
E. W. Lewis and G. W. Hillyard
1891 W. Baddeley and H. Baddeley
J. Pim and F. O. Stoker
1892 H. S. Barlow and E. W. Lewis
W. Baddeley and H. Baddeley
1893 J. Pim and F. O. Stoker
E. W. Lewis and H. S. Barlow
1894 W. Baddeley and H. Baddeley
H. S. Barlow and C. H. Martin
1895 W. Baddeley and H. Baddeley
E. W. Lewis and W. V. Eaves
1896 W. Baddeley and H. Baddeley
R. F. Doherty and H. A. Nisbet
1897 R. F. Doherty and H. L. Doherty
W. Baddeley and H. Baddeley
1898 R. F. Doherty and H. L. Doherty
H. A. Nisbet and C. Hobart
1899 R. F. Doherty and H. L. Doherty
H. A. Nisbet and C. Hobart
1900 R. F. Doherty and H. L. Doherty
H. Roper Barrett and H. A. Nisbet
1901 R. F. Doherty and H. L. Doherty
Dwight Davis and Holcombe Ward
1902 S. H. Smith and F. L. Riseley
R. F. Doherty and H. L. Doherty
1903 R. F. Doherty and H. L. Doherty
S. H. Smith and F. L. Riseley
1904 R. F. Doherty and H. L. Doherty
S. H. Smith and F. L. Riseley
1905 R. F. Doherty and H. L. Doherty
S. H. Smith and F. L. Riseley
1906 S. H. Smith and F. L. Riseley
R. F. Doherty and H. L. Doherty
1907 N. E. Brooks and A. F. Wilding
B. C. Wright and K. H. Behr
1908 A. F. Wilding and M. J. G. Ritchie
A. W. Gore and H. Roper Barrett
1909 A. W. Gore and H. Roper Barrett
S. N. Doust and H. A. Parker
1910 A. F. Wilding and M. J. G. Ritchie
A. W. Gore and H. Roper Barrett
1911 M. Decugis and A. H. Gobert
M. J. G. Ritchie and A. F. Wilding
1912 H. Roper Barrett and C. P. Dixon
M. Decugis and A. H. Gobert
1913 H. Roper Barrett and C. P. Dixon
F. W. Rahe and H. Kleinschroth
1914 N. E. Brookes and A. F. Wilding
H. Roper Barrett and C. P. Dixon
1919 R. V. Thomas and P. O'Hara-Wood
R. Lycett and R. W. Heath
1920 R. N. Williams and C. S. Garland
A. R. F. Kingscote and J. C. Parke
1921 R. Lycett and M. Woosnam
F. G. Lowe and A. H. Lowe
1922 R. Lycett and J. O. Anderson
G. L. Patterson and P. O'Hara-Wood
1923 R. Lycett and L. A. Godfree
Count de Gomar and E. Flaquer
1924 F. T. Hunter and V. Richards
R. N. Williams and W. M. Washburn
1925 J. Borotra and R. Lacoste
J. Hennessey and R. Casey
1926 H. Cochet and J. Brugnon
V. Richards and H. Kinsey
1927 F. T. Hunter and W. T. Tilden
J. Brugnon and H. Cochet
1928 H. Cochet and J. Brugnon
G. L. Patterson and J. B. Hawkes
1929 W. Allison and J. Van Ryn
J. C. Gregory and I. G. Collins
1930 W. Allison and J. Van Ryn
J. H. Doeg and G. M. Lott
1931 G. M Lott and J. Van Ryn
H. Cochet and J. Brugnon
1932 J. Borotra and J. Brugnon
G. P. Hughes and F. J. Perry
1933 J. Borotra and J. Brugnon
R. Nunoi and J. Satoh
1934 G. M. Lott and L. R. Stoefen
J. Borotra and J. Brugnon
1935 J. H. Crawford and A. K. Quist
W. Allison and J. Van Ryn
1936 G. P. Hughes and C. R. D. Tuckey
C. E. Hare and F. H. D. Wilde
1937 J. D. Budge and G. Mako
G. P. Hughes and C. R. D. Tuckey
1938 J. D. Budge and G. Mako
H. Henkel and G. von Metaxa
1939 R. L. Riggs and E. T. Cooke
C. E. Hare and F. H. D. Wilde
1946 T. Brown and J. Kramer
G. E. Brown and D. Pails
1947 R. Falkenburg and J. Kramer
A. J. Mottram and O. W. Sidwell
1948 J. E. Bromwich and F. A. Sedgman
T. Brown and G. Mulloy
1949 R. Gonzales and F. Parker
G. Mulloy and F. R. Schroeder
1950 J. E. Bromwich and A. K. Quist
G. E. Brown and O. W. Sidwell
1951 K. McGregor and F. A. Sedgman
J. Drobny and E. W. Sturgess
1952 K. McGregor and F. A. Sedgman
V. Seixas and E. W. Sturgess
1953 L. A. Hoad and K. R. Rosewall
R. N. Hartwig and M. G. Rose
1954 R. N. Hartwig and M. G. Rose
V. Seixas and T. Trabert
1955 R. N. Hartwig and L. A. Hoad
N. A. Fraser and K. R. Rosewall
1956 L. A. Hoad and K. R. Rosewall
N. Pietrangeli and O. Sirola
1957 G. Mulloy and B. Patty
N. A. Fraser and L. A. Hoad
1958 S. Davidson and U. Schmidt
A. J. Cooper and N. A. Fraser
1959 R. Emerson and N. A. Fraser
R. Laver and R. Mark
1960 R. H. Osuna and R. D. Ralston
M. G. Davies and R. K. Wilson
1961 R. Emerson and N. A. Fraser
R. A. J. Hewitt and F. S. Stolle
1962 R. A. J. Hewitt and F. S. Stolle
B. Jovanovic and N. Pilic
1963 R. H. Osuna and A. Palafox
J. C. Barclay and P. Darmon
1964 R. A. J. Hewitt and F. S. Stolle
R. Emerson and K. N. Fletcher
1965 J. D. Newcombe and A. D. Roche
K. N. Fletcher and R. A. J. Hewitt
1966 K. N. Fletcher and J. D. Newcombe
W. W. Bowrey and O. K. Davidson
1967 R. A. J. Hewitt and F. D. McMillan
R. Emerson and K. N. Fletcher
1968 J. D. Newcombe and A. D. Roche
K. R. Rosewall and F. S. Stolle
1969 J. D. Newcombe and A. D. Roche
T. S. Okker and M. C. Reissen
1970 J. D. Newcombe and A. D. Roche
K. R. Rosewall and F. S. Stolle
1971 R. S. Emerson and R. G. Laver
A. R. Ashe and R. D. Ralston
1972 R. A. J. Hewitt and F. D. McMillan
S. R. Smith and E. J. van Dillen
1973 J. S. Connors and I. Nastase
J. R. Cooper and N. A. Fraser
1974 J. D. Newcombe and A. D. Roche
R. C. Lutz and S. R. Smith
1975 V. Gerulaitis and A. Mayer
C. Dowdeswell and A. J. Stone
1976 B. E. Gottfried and R. Ramirez
R. L. Case and G. Masters
1977 R. L. Case and G. Masters
J. G. Alexander and P. C. Dent
1978 R. A. J. Hewitt and F. D. McMillan
P. Fleming and J. P. McEnroe
1979 P. Fleming and J. P. McEnroe
B. E. Gottfried and R. Ramirez
1980 P. McNamara and P. McNamee
R. C. Lutz and S. R. Smith
1981 P. Fleming and J. P. McEnroe
R. C. Lutz and S. R. Smith
1982 P. McNamara and P. McNamee
P. Fleming and J. P. McEnroe
1983 P. Fleming and J. P. McEnroe
T. E. Gullikson and T. R. Gullikson
1984 P. Fleming and J. P. McEnroe
P. Cash and P. McNamee
1985 H. P. Guenthardt and B. Taroczy
P. Cash and J. B. Fitzgerald
1986 J. Nystrom and M. Wilander
G. Donnelly and P. Fleming
1987 K. Flach and R. Seguso
S. Casal and E. Sanchez
1988 K. Flach and R. Seguso
J. B. Fitzgerald and A. Jarryd
1989 J. B. Fitzgerald and A. Jarryd
R. Leach and J. Pugh
1990 R. Leach and J. Pugh
P. Aldrich and D. T. Visser
1991 J. B. Fitzgerald and A. Jarryd
J. Frana and L. Lavalle
1992 J. P. McEnroe and M. Stich
J. Grabb and R. A. Reneberg
1993 T. A. Woodbridge and M. Woodforde
G. Connell and P. Galbraith
1994 T. A. Woodbridge and M. Woodforde
G. Connell and P. Galbraith
1995 T. A. Woodbridge and M. Woodforde
R. Leach and S. Melville
1996 T. A. Woodbridge and M. Woodforde
B. Black and G. Connell
1997 T. A. Woodbridge and M. Woodforde
J. Eltingh and P. Haarhuis
1998 J. Eltingh and P. Haarhuis
T. A. Woodbridge and M. Woodforde
1999 M. Bhupathi and L. Paes
P. Haarhuis and J. Palmer
2000 T. A. Woodbridge and M. Woodforde
P. Haarhuis and S. Stolle
2001 D. Johnson and J. Palmer
J. Novak & D. Rikl

LADIES' DOUBLES

1913 Mrs. R. J. McNair and Miss D. P. Boothby
Mrs. A. Sterry and Mrs. Lambert Chambers
1914 Miss E. Ryan and Miss A. M. Morton
Mrs. D. R. Larcombe and Mrs. F. J. Hannam
1919 Mlle. S. Lenglen and Miss E. Ryan
Mrs. Lambert Chambers and Mrs. D. R. Larcombe
1920 Mlle. S. Lenglen and Miss E. Ryan
Mrs. Lambert Chambers and Mrs. D. R. Larcombe
1921 Mlle. S. Lenglen and Miss E. Ryan
Mrs. A. E. Beamish and Mrs. G. E. Peacock
1922 Mlle. S. Lenglen and Miss E. Ryan
Mrs. A. D. Stocks and Miss K. McKane
1923 Mlle. S. Lenglen and Miss E. Ryan
Miss J. Austin and Miss E. L. Colyer
1924 Mrs. H. Wightman and Miss H. Wills
Mrs. B. C. Covell and Miss K. McKane
1925 Mlle. S. Lenglen and Miss E. Ryan
Mrs. A. V. Bridge and Mrs. C. G. McIlquham
1926 Miss E. Ryan and Miss M. K. Browne
Mrs. L. A. Godfree and Miss E. L. Colyer
1927 Miss H. Wills and Miss E. Ryan
Miss E. L. Heine and Mrs. G. E. Peacock
1928 Mrs. Holcroft-Watson and Miss P. Saunders
Miss E. H. Harvey and Miss E. Bennett
1929 Mrs. Holcroft-Watson and Mrs. L.R.C. Michell
Mrs. B. C. Covell and Mrs. D. C. Shepherd-Barron
1930 Mrs. F. S. Moody and Miss E. Ryan
Miss E. Cross and Miss S. Palfrey
1931 Mrs.D.C. Shepherd-Barron and Miss P.E. Mudford
Mlle. D. Metaxa and Mlle. J. Sigart
1932 Mlle. D. Metaxa and Mlle. J. Sigart
Miss E. Ryan and Miss H. H. Jacobs
1933 Mme. R. Mathieu and Miss E. Ryan
Miss F. James and Miss A. M. Yorke
1934 Mme. R. Mathieu and Miss E. Ryan
Mrs. D. Andrus and Mme. S. Henrotin
1935 Miss F. James and Miss K. E. Stammers
Mme. R. Mathieu and Frau. S. Sperling
1936 Miss F. James and Miss K. E. Stammers
Mrs. S. P. Fabyan and Miss H. H. Jacobs
1937 Mme. R. Mathieu and Miss A. M. Yorke
Mrs. M. R. King and Mrs. J. B. Pittman
1938 Mrs. S. P. Fabyan and Miss A. Marble
Mme. R. Mathieu and Miss A. M. Yorke
1939 Mrs S. P. Fabyan and Miss A. Marble
Miss H. H. Jacobs and Miss A. M. Yorke
1946 Miss L. Brough and Miss M. Osborne
Miss P. Betz and Miss D. Hart
1947 Miss D. Hart and Mrs. P. C. Todd
Miss L. Brough and Miss M. Osborne
1948 Miss L. Brough and Mrs. W. du Pont
Miss D. Hart and Mrs. P. C. Todd
1949 Miss L. Brough and Mrs. W. du Pont
Miss G. Moran and Mrs. P. C. Todd
1950 Miss L. Brough and Mrs. W. du Pont
Miss S. Fry and Miss D. Hart
1951 Miss S. Fry and Miss D. Hart
Miss L. Brough and Mrs. W. du Pont
1952 Miss S. Fry and Miss D. Hart
Miss L. Brough and Miss M. Connolly
1953 Miss S. Fry and Miss D. Hart
Miss M. Connolly and Miss J. Sampson
1954 Miss L. Brough and Mrs. W. du Pont
Miss S. Fry and Miss D. Hart
1955 Miss A. Mortimer and Miss J. A. Shilcock
Miss S. J. Bloomer and Miss P. E. Ward
1956 Miss A. Buxton and Miss A. Gibson
Miss F. Muller and Miss D. G. Seeney
1957 Miss A. Gibson and Miss D. R. Hard
Mrs. K. Hawton and Mrs. T. D. Long
1958 Miss M. E. Bueno and Miss A. Gibson
Mrs. W. du Pont and Miss M. Varner
1959 Miss J. Arth and Miss D. R. Hard
Mrs. J. G. Fleitz and Miss C. C. Truman
1960 Miss M. E. Bueno and Miss D. R. Hard
Miss S. Reynolds and Miss R. Schuurman
1961 Miss K. Hantze and Miss B. J. Moffitt
Miss J. Lehane and Miss M. Smith
1962 Miss B. J. Moffitt and Mrs. J. R. Susman
Mrs. L. E. G. Price and Miss R. Schuurman
1963 Miss M. E. Bueno and Miss D. R. Hard
Miss R. A. Ebbern and Miss M. Smith
1964 Miss M. Smith and Miss L. R. Turner
Miss B. J. Moffitt and Mrs. J. R. Susman
1965 Miss M. E. Bueno and Miss B. J. Moffitt
Miss F. Durr and Miss J. Lieffrig
1966 Miss M. E. Bueno and Miss N. Richey
Miss M. Smith and Miss J. A. M. Tegart
1967 Miss R. Casals and Mrs. L. W. King
Miss M. E. Bueno and Miss N. Richey
1968 Miss R. Casals and Mrs. L. W. King
Miss F. Durr and Mrs. P. F. Jones
1969 Mrs. B. M. Court and Miss J. A. M. Tegart
Miss P. S. A. Hogan and Miss M. Michel
1970 Miss R. Casals and Mrs. L. W. King
Miss F. Durr and Miss S. V. Wade
1971 Miss R. Casals and Mrs. L. W. King
Mrs. B. M. Court and Miss E. F. Goolagong
1972 Mrs. L. W. King and Miss B. F. Stove
Mrs. D. E. Dalton and Miss F. Durr
1973 Miss R. Casals and Mrs. L. W. King
Miss F. Durr and Miss B. F. Stove
1974 Miss E. F. Goolagong and Miss M. Michel
Miss H. F. Gourlay and Miss K. M. Krantzcke
1975 Miss A. Kiyomura and Miss K. Sawamatsu
Miss F. Durr and Miss B. F. Stove
1976 Miss C. M. Evert and Miss M. Navratilova
Mrs. L. W. King and Miss B. F. Stove
1977 Mrs. H. F. Gourlay Cawley and Miss J. C. Russell
Miss M. Navratilova and Miss B. F. Stove
1978 Mrs. G. E. Reid and Miss. W. M. Turnbull
Miss M. Jausovec and Miss V. Ruzici
1979 Mrs. L. W. King and Miss M. Navratilova
Miss B. F. Stove and Miss W. M. Turnbull
1980 Miss K. Jordan and Miss A. E. Smith
Miss R. Casals and Miss W. M. Turnbull
1981 Miss M. Navratilova and Miss P. H. Shriver
Miss K. Jordan and Miss A. E. Smith
1982 Miss M. Navratilova and Miss P. H. Shriver
Miss K. Jordan and Miss A. E. Smith
1983 Miss M. Navratilova and Miss P. H. Shriver
Miss R. Casals and Miss W. M. Turnbull
1984 Miss M. Navratilova and Miss P. H. Shriver
Miss K. Jordan and Miss A. E. Smith
1985 Miss K. Jordan and Mrs. P. D. Smylie
Miss M. Navratilova and Miss P. H. Shriver
1986 Miss M. Navratilova and Miss P. H. Shriver
Miss H. Mandlikova and Miss W. M. Turnbull
1987 Miss C. Kohde-Kilsch and Miss H. Sukova
Miss B. Nagelsen and Mrs. P. D. Smylie
1988 Miss S. Graf and Miss G. Sabatini
Miss L. Savchenko and Miss N. Zvereva
1989 Miss J. Novotna and Miss H. Sukova
Miss L. Savchenko and Miss N. Zvereva
1990 Miss J. Novotna and Miss H. Sukova
Miss K. Jordan and Mrs. P. D. Smylie
1991 Miss L. Savchenko and Miss N. Zvereva
Miss G. Fernandez and Miss J. Novotna
1992 Miss G. Fernandez and Miss N. Zvereva
Miss J. Novotna and Mrs. L. Savchenko-Neiland
1993 Miss G. Fernandez and Miss N. Zvereva
Mrs. L. Neiland and Miss J. Novotna
1994 Miss G. Fernandez and Miss N. Zvereva
Miss J. Novotna and Miss A. Sanchez Vicario
1995 Miss J. Novotna and Miss A. Sanchez Vicario
Miss G. Fernandez and Miss N. Zvereva
1996 Miss M. Hingis and Miss H. Sukova
Miss M. J. McGrath and Mrs. L. Neiland
1997 Miss G. Fernandez and Miss N. Zvereva
Miss N. J. Arendt and Miss M. M. Bollegraf
1998 Miss M. Hingis and Miss J. Novotna
Miss L. A. Davenport and Miss N. Zvereva
1999 Miss L. A. Davenport and Miss C. Morariu
Miss M. de Swardt and Miss E. Tatarkova
2000 Miss S. Williams and Miss V. Williams
Mrs J. Halard-Decugis and Miss A. Sugiyama
2001 Miss L. M. Raymond and Miss R. P. Stubbs
Miss K. Clijsters and Miss A. Sugiyama

MIXED DOUBLES

1913 Hope Crisp and Mrs. C. O. Tuckey *J. C. Parke and Mrs. D. R. Larcombe*	1937 J. D. Budge and Miss A. Marble *Y. Petra and Mme. R. Mathieu*	1963 K. N. Fletcher and Miss M. Smith *R. A. J. Hewitt and Miss D. R. Hard*	1983 J. M. Lloyd and Miss W. M. Turnbull *S. Denton and Mrs. L. W. King*

1913 Hope Crisp and Mrs. C. O. Tuckey
J. C. Parke and Mrs. D. R. Larcombe
1914 J. C. Parke and Mrs. D.R. Larcombe
A. F.Wilding and Mlle. M. Broquedis
1919 R. Lycett and Miss E. Ryan
A. D. Prebble and Mrs. Lambert Chambers
1920 G. L. Patterson and Mlle. S. Lenglen
R. Lycett and Miss E. Ryan
1921 R. Lycett and Miss E. Ryan
M. Woosnam and Mrs. P. L. Howkins
1922 P. O'Hara-Wood and Mlle. S. Lenglen
R. Lycett and Miss E. Ryan
1923 R. Lycett and Miss E. Ryan
L. S. Deane and Mrs. D. C. Shepherd-Barron
1924 J. B. Gilbert and Miss K. McKane
L. A. Godfree and Mrs. D. C. Shepherd-Barron
1925 J. Borotra and Mlle. S. Lenglen
H. L. de Morpurgo and Miss E. Ryan
1926 L. A. Godfree and Mrs. L. A. Godfree
H. Kinsey and Miss M. K. Browne
1927 F.T. Hunter and Miss E. Ryan
L. A. Godfree and Mrs. L. A. Godfree
1928 P. D. B. Spence and Miss E. Ryan
J. Crawford and Miss D. Akhurst
1929 F.T. Hunter and Miss H. Wills
I. G. Collins and Miss J. Fry
1930 J. H. Crawford and Miss E. Ryan
D. Prenn and Fraulein H. Krahwinkel
1931 G. M. Lott and Mrs L. A. Harper
I. G. Collins and Miss J. C. Ridley
1932 E. Maier and Miss E. Ryan
H. C. Hopman and Mlle. J. Sigart
1933 G. von Cramm and Fraulein H. Krahwinkel
N. G. Farquharson and Miss M. Heeley
1934 R. Miki and Miss D. E. Round
H. W.Austin and Mrs D. C. Shepherd-Barron
1935 F. J. Perry and Miss D. E. Round
H. C. Hopman and Mrs. H. C. Hopman
1936 F. J. Perry and Miss D. E. Round
J. D. Budge and Miss S. P. Fabyan

1937 J. D. Budge and Miss A. Marble
Y. Petra and Mme. R. Mathieu
1938 J. D. Budge and Miss A. Marble
H. Henkel and Mrs. S. P. Fabyan
1939 R. L. Riggs and Miss A. Marble
F. H. D.Wilde and Miss N. B. Brown
1946 T. Brown and Miss L. Brough
G. E. Brown and Miss D. Bundy
1947 J. E. Bromwich and Miss L. Brough
C. F. Long and Mrs. N. M. Bolton
1948 J. E. Bromwich and Miss L. Brough
F. A. Sedgman and Miss D. Hart
1949 E. W. Sturgess and Mrs. S. P. Summers
J. E. Bromwich and Miss L. Brough
1950 E. W. Sturgess and Miss L. Brough
G. E. Brown and Mrs. P. C. Todd
1951 F. A. Sedgman and Miss D. Hart
M. G. Rose and Mrs. N. M. Bolton
1952 F. A. Sedgman and Miss D. Hart
E. Morea and Mrs. T. D. Long
1953 V. Seixas and Miss D. Hart
E. Morea and Miss S. Fry
1954 V. Seixas and Miss D. Hart
K. R. Rosewall and Mrs. W. du Pont
1955 V. Seixas and Miss D. Hart
E. Morea and Miss L. Brough
1956 V. Seixas and Miss S. Fry
G. Mulloy and Miss A. Gibson
1957 M. G. Rose and Miss D. R. Hard
N. A. Fraser and Miss A. Gibson
1958 R. N. Howe and Miss L. Coghlan
K. Nielsen and Miss A. Gibson
1959 R. Laver and Miss D. R. Hard
N. A. Fraser and Miss M. E. Bueno
1960 R. Laver and Miss D. R. Hard
R. N. Howe and Miss M. E. Bueno
1961 F. S. Stolle and Miss L. R. Turner
R. N. Howe and Miss E. Buding
1962 N. A. Fraser and Mrs. W. du Pont
R. D. Ralston and Miss A. S. Haydon

1963 K. N. Fletcher and Miss M. Smith
R. A. J. Hewitt and Miss D. R. Hard
1964 F. S. Stolle and Miss L. R. Turner
K. N. Fletcher and Miss M. Smith
1965 K. N. Fletcher and Miss M. Smith
A. D. Roche and Miss J. A. M. Tegart
1966 K. N. Fletcher and Miss M. Smith
R. D. Ralston and Mrs. L. W. King
1967 O. K. Davidson and Mrs. L. W. King
K. N. Fletcher and Miss M. E. Bueno
1968 K. N. Fletcher and Mrs. B. M. Court
A. Metreveli and Miss O. Morozova
1969 F. S. Stolle and Miss P. F. Jones
A. D. Roche and Miss J. A. M. Tegart
1970 I. Nastase and Miss R. Casals
A. Metreveli and Miss O. Morozova
1971 O. K. Davidson and Mrs. L. W. King
M. C. Riessen and Mrs. B. M. Court
1972 I. Nastase and Miss R. Casals
K. G. Warwick and Miss E. F. Goolagong
1973 O. K. Davidson and Mrs. L. W. King
R. Ramirez and Miss J. S. Newberry
1974 O. K. Davidson and Mrs. L. W. King
M. J. Farrell and Miss L. J. Charles
1975 M. C. Riessen and Mrs. B. M. Court
A. J. Stone and Miss B. F. Stove
1976 A. D. Roche and Miss F. Durr
R. L. Stockton and Miss R. Casals
1977 R. A. J. Hewitt and Miss G. R. Stevens
F. D. McMillan and Miss B. F. Stove
1978 F. D. McMillan and Miss B. F. Stove
R. O. Ruffels and Mrs. L. W. King
1979 R. A. J. Hewitt and Miss G. R. Stevens
F. D. McMillan and Miss B. F. Stove
1980 J. R. Austin and Miss T. Austin
M. R. Edmondson and Miss D. L. Fromholtz
1981 F. D. McMillan and Miss B. F. Stove
J. R. Austin and Miss T. Austin
1982 K. Curren and Miss A. E. Smith
J. M. Lloyd and Miss W. M. Turnbull

1983 J. M. Lloyd and Miss W. M. Turnbull
S. Denton and Mrs. L. W. King
1984 J. M. Lloyd and Miss W. M. Turnbull
S. Denton and Miss K. Jordan
1985 P. McNamee and Miss M. Navratilova
J. B. Fitzgerald and Mrs. P. D. Smylie
1986 K. Flach and Miss K. Jordan
H. P. Guenthardt and Miss M. Navratilova
1987 M. J. Bates and Miss J. M. Durie
D. Cahill and Miss N. Provis
1988 S. E. Stewart and Miss Z. L. Garrison
K. Jones and Mrs. S. W. Magers
1989 J. Pugh and Miss J. Novotna
M. Kratzmann and Miss J. M. Byrne
1990 R. Leach and Miss Z. L. Garrison
J. B. Fitzgerald and Mrs P. D. Smylie
1991 J. B. Fitzgerald and Mrs. P. D. Smylie
J. Pugh and Miss N. Zvereva
1992 C. Suk and Mrs L. Savchenko-Neiland
J. Eltingh and Miss M. Oremans
1993 M. Woodforde and Miss M. Navratilova
T. Nijssen and Miss M. M. Bollegraf
1994 T. A. Woodbridge and Miss H. Sukova
T. J. Middleton and Miss L. M. McNeil
1995 J. Stark and Miss M. Navratilova
C. Suk and Miss G. Fernandez
1996 C. Suk and Miss H. Sukova
M. Woodforde and Mrs. L. Neiland
1997 C. Suk and Miss H. Sukova
A. Olhovskiy and Mrs L. Neiland
1998 M. Mirnyi and Miss S. Williams
M. Bhupathi and Miss M. Lucic
1999 L. Paes and Miss L.M. Raymond
J. Bjorkman and Miss A. Kournikova
2000 D. Johnson and Miss K. Po
L. Hewitt and Miss K. Clijsters
2001 L. Friedl and Miss D. Hantuchova
M. Bryan and Mrs L. Huber

THE JUNIOR CHAMPIONSHIP ROLL

BOYS' SINGLES

1947 K. Nielsen (Denmark)
1948 S. Stockenberg (Sweden)
1949 S. Stockenberg (Sweden)
1950 J.A.T. Horn (G.B.)
1951 J. Kupferburger (S.A.)
1952 R. K. Wilson (G.B.)
1953 W. A. Knight (G.B.)
1954 R. Krishnan (India)
1955 M. P. Hann (G.B.)
1956 R. Holmberg (U.S.A.)
1957 J. I. Tattersall (G.B.)
1958 E. Buchholz (U.S.A.)
1959 T. Lejus (U.S.S.R.)
1960 A. R. Mandelstam (S.A.)

1961 C. E. Graebner (U.S.A.)
1962 S. Matthews (G.B.)
1963 N. Kalogeropoulos (Greece)
1964 I. El Shafei (U.A.R.)
1965 V. Korotkov (U.S.S.R.)
1966 V. Korotkov (U.S.S.R.)
1967 M. Orantes (Spain)
1968 J. G. Alexander (Australia)
1969 B. Bertram (S.A.)
1970 B. Bertram (S.A.)
1971 R. Kreiss (U.S.A.)
1972 B. Borg (Sweden)
1973 W. Martin (U.S.A.)
1974 W. Martin (U.S.A.)

1975 C. J. Lewis (N.Z.)
1976 H. Guenthardt (Switzerland)
1977 V. A. Winitsky (U.S.A.)
1978 I. Lendl (Czechoslovakia)
1979 R. Krishnan (India)
1980 T. Tulasne (France)
1981 M. W. Anger (U.S.A.)
1982 P. Cash (Australia)
1983 S. Edberg (Sweden)
1984 M.Kratzmann (Australia)
1985 L. Lavalle (Mexico)
1986 E. Velez (Mexico)
1987 D. Nargiso (Italy)
1988 N. Pereira (Venezuela)

1989 N. Kulti (Sweden)
1990 L. Paes (India)
1991 T. Enquist (Sweden)
1992 D. Skoch (Czechoslovakia)
1993 R. Sabau (Romania)
1994 S. Humphries (U.S.A.)
1995 O. Mutis (France)
1996 V.Voltchkov (Belarus)
1997 W.Whitehouse (South Africa)
1998 R. Federer (Switzerland)
1999 J. Melzer (Austria)
2000 N. Mahut (France)
2001 R. Valent (Switzerland)

BOYS' DOUBLES

1982 P. Cash and J. Frawley
1983 M. Kratzmann and S.Youl
1984 R. Brown and R. Weiss
1985 A. Moreno and J.Yzaga
1986 T. Carbonell and P. Korda

1987 J. Stoltenberg and T. Woodbridge
1988 J. Stoltenberg and T. Woodbridge
1989 J. Palmer and J. Stark
1990 S. Lareau and S. Leblanc
1991 K. Alami and G. Rusedski

1992 S. Baldas and S. Draper
1993 S. Downs and J. Greenhalgh
1994 B. Ellwood and M. Philippoussis
1995 M. Lee and J.M. Trotman
1996 D. Bracciali and J. Robichaud

1997 L. Horna and N. Massu
1998 R. Federer and O. Rochus
1999 G. Coria and D. Nalbandian
2000 D. Coene and K.Vliegen
2001 F. Dancevic and G. Lapentti

GIRLS' SINGLES

1947 Miss B. Domken (Belgium)
1948 Miss O. Miskova (Czechoslovakia)
1949 Miss C. Mercelis (Belgium)
1950 Miss L. Cornell (G.B.)
1951 Miss L. Cornell (G.B.)
1952 Miss ten Bosch (Netherlands)
1953 Miss D. Kilian (S.A.)
1954 Miss V.A. Pitt (G.B.)
1955 Miss S. M. Armstrong (G.B.)
1956 Miss A. S. Haydon (G.B.)
1957 Miss M. Arnold (U.S.A.)
1958 Miss S. M. Moore (U.S.A.)
1959 Miss J. Cross (S.A.)
1960 Miss K. Hantze (U.S.A.)

1961 Miss G. Baksheeva (U.S.S.R.)
1962 Miss G. Baksheeva (U.S.S.R.)
1963 Miss D. M. Salfati (France)
1964 Miss P. Bartkowicz (U.S.A.)
1965 Miss O. Morozova (U.S.S.R.)
1966 Miss B. Lindstrom (Finland)
1967 Miss J. Salome (Netherlands)
1968 Miss K. Pigeon (U.S.A.)
1969 Miss K. Sawamatsu (Japan)
1970 Miss S. Walsh (U.S.A.)
1971 Miss M. Kroschina (U.S.S.R.)
1972 Miss I. Kloss (S.A.)
1973 Miss A. Kiyomura (U.S.A.)
1974 Miss M. Jausovec (Yugoslavia)

1975 Miss N.Y. Chmyreva (U.S.S.R.)
1976 Miss N.Y. Chmyreva (U.S.S.R.)
1977 Miss L. Antonoplis (U.S.A.)
1978 Miss T. Austin (U.S.A.)
1979 Miss M. L. Piatek (U.S.A.)
1980 Miss D. Freeman (Australia)
1981 Miss Z. Garrison (U.S.A.)
1982 Miss C. Tanvier (France)
1983 Miss P. Paradis (France)
1984 Miss A. N. Croft (G.B.)
1985 Miss A. Holikova (Czechoslovakia)
1986 Miss N. Zvereva (U.S.S.R.)
1987 Miss N. Zvereva (U.S.S.R.)
1988 Miss B. Schultz (Netherlands)

1989 Miss A. Strnadova (Czechoslavakia)
1990 Miss A. Strnadova (Czechoslavakia)
1991 Miss B. Rittner (Germany)
1992 Miss C. Rubin (U.S.A.)
1993 Miss N. Feber (Belgium)
1994 Miss M. Hingis (Switzerland)
1995 Miss A. Olsza (Poland)
1996 Miss A. Mauresmo (France)
1997 Miss C. Black (Zimbabwe)
1998 Miss K. Srebotnik (Slovenia)
1999 Miss I. Tulyagnova (Uzbekhistan)
2000 Miss M. E. Salerni (Argentina)
2001 Miss A. Widjaja (Indonesia)

GIRLS' DOUBLES

1982 Miss B. Herr and Miss P. Barg
1983 Miss P. Fendick and Miss P. Hy
1984 Miss C. Kuhlman and Miss S. Rehe
1985 Miss L. Field and Miss J. Thompson
1986 Miss M. Jaggard and Miss L. O'Neill

1987 Miss N. Medvedeva and Miss N. Zvereva
1988 Miss J.A. Faull and Miss R. McQuillan
1989 Miss J. Capriati and Miss M. McGrath
1990 Miss K. Habsudova and Miss A. Strnadova
1991 Miss C. Barclay and Miss L. Zaltz

1992 Miss M. Avotins and Miss L. McShea
1993 Miss L. Courtois and Miss N. Feber
1994 Miss E. De Villiers and Miss E. E. Jelfs
1995 Miss C. Black and Miss A. Olsza
1996 Miss O. Barabanschikova and Miss A. Mauresmo

1997 Miss C. Black and Miss I. Selyutina
1998 Miss E. Dyrberg and Miss J. Kostanic
1999 Miss D. Bedanova and Miss M.E. Salerni
2000 Miss I. Gaspar and Miss T. Perebiynis
2001 Miss G. Dulko and Miss A. Harkleroad